Dedicated to anyone who's
ever heard the three worst words
in the English language:

'Let's be friends'

. . . And to anyone who's ever had
the intelligence to respond:

'That's nice – but
at this point, I don't need
any more friends.'

BRUCE FEIRSTEIN

Nice Guys Sleep Alone

Dating in the Difficult Eighties

Illustrated by Shary Flenniken

Fontana/Collins

First published in 1987 by Fontana Paperbacks
8 Grafton Street, London W1X 3LA

Made and printed in Great Britain
by William Collins Sons & Co. Ltd, Glasgow

An excerpt of this book originally appeared in *Playboy*.

'Contracting A Love Affair' was first published in *New York* Magazine May 4, 1981.

The chapter 'Why You Should Never Date a Yuppie' was first published in *The New York Times Magazine*.

Grateful acknowledgement is made for permission to quote from the following song lyrics:

'Chapel of Love' Reprinted by permission of Warner Bros. Music. Composed by Jeff Barry, Ellie Greenwich, and Phil Spector. Copyright © by Trio Music Co. Inc. and Mother Bertha Music Inc.

'Think!' Reprinted by permission of Fourteenth Hour Music. Words and music by Ted White and Aretha Franklin. Copyright © 1968 by Fourteenth Hour Music

'Leader of the Pack' Copyright © 1964 by EMI Music Publishing Ltd., Tender Tunes Music Co. and Trio Music Co., Inc. All rights for the U.S. and Canada controlled by Screen Gems-EMI Music Inc. All rights reserved. Used by permission.

'Will You Still Love Me Tomorrow' Copyright © 1960, 1961, Screen Gems-EMI Music Inc. All rights reserved. Used by permission.

For my sister, and best friend, Andrea.

To some extent, all books like these are collaborative efforts.

Aside from apologizing to every woman I've ever dated, I'd like to thank Ruth and Jake Bloom (the very definition of nice people); my editors at Dell, the talented and insightful Gary Luke and the ever-patient Susan Moldow; my editor in London, Michael Fishwick; Shary Flenniken; Stephen and Caroline Kass (the East Coast definition of nice people); and the much-respected and always supportive Lois Wallace.

Additional thanks are due: Sara Altshul; Al Burton; Ann Busby (for the WASP point of view); Lee and Gita Caplin (for their encouragement dinners); George and Helen Feirstein (because they'd kill me if I didn't); Roberta Finke (my stand-in wife of twenty years, from room 226 at SOJH to Saturday nights at the summer palace); Candice Hanson; Judy Hofflund; Marcia, Mark and Amanda Lewis-Smith (for the apartment, especially the fish); Penny Marshall; Dr Alan Matarasso (friend, confidant, plastic surgeon); my family at Perlbinder International Airways ('Our aim is to get you off'); Marilyn Suzanne Miller; Stephanie Pressman; Miss Katherine Reback (attractive, intelligent *and* stylish – a triple treat, the most precious of combinations); Jonathan Roberts; Robin Schultz; Joel Silver (who, surpassing James Brown, is truly the hardest-working man in show business); Melissa Steinberg; Jay Weiss and K.T.; Pat Zacharian; and finally, the Zweibel family.

Needless to say, 'Nice Guys' is a work of fiction, and any resemblance to persons living or dead is purely coincidental.

But if the shoe fits, why not wear it?

B.F.
Los Angeles
April 24th, 1986

Nice Guys
Sleep Alone

INTRODUCTION

Sam Spade in the Eighties: *The Big Sleep* Meets *The Big Chill*

I was halfway into a pack of Marlboros when she walked into my office. It had been raining since the beginning of the decade, and I was not only tired but wet.

'Why don't you take a load off those leg warmers and have a seat on the modular couch,' I told her, but she didn't move from the doorway.

'Sam, we have to talk.'

'About what, precious?'

'About us,' she sighed. 'About our relationship.'

I looked her up and down. Sure, she was beautiful. Sure, she was wearing the kind of legs that went from Harrods to Harvey Nichols and back . . .

But the way I see it, a guy's got to draw the line when his date sleeps with his partner.

'I'm throwing you over, angel,' I told her. 'We may have had something once, but it's finished.'

'But, Sam,' she cried. 'How can you say that? How can you act this way after the time we've spent together?'

Sitting there, our first night came rushing back, hitting me in the face like a hot towel at a sushi bar. Sure she'd worn perfume that screamed 'Two tickets to Paris. Concorde.' Sure, she had a voice that clung to the walls like cheap smoke from a charcoal grill. And sure, she had a smile that said it all: cold, hard, and fast, like the front grille of a Baby Merc . . .

13

But a guy just can't turn the other cheek when his date sleeps with his partner.

And his Mercedes-Benz mechanic.

And his sushi chef.

I lit another cigarette.

'You smoke too much,' she said, and I began to fume.

'You have no right to say that,' I yelled at her. 'You never played straight with me for more than five minutes in this relationship. First you slept with Fenton, then with Henry, then with Charlie. What did you think? I wouldn't find out? I'm sending you over, darling, I won't play the sap for you anymore. You're getting in your bed tonight, and you're getting in alone.'

'Don't – don't say that!' she moaned. 'Those other people weren't important. You're the only one I ever cared about. But you were only interested in your career. You said you couldn't make a commitment.' She began to cry. 'You've got to give me another chance. I know we could make it work.'

I walked around the desk.

'Sure, we could give it another chance, angel. But we both know it would be wrong. We may not regret it today, or when we wake up tomorrow, but sooner or later we'd regret it for the rest of our lives. The truth is we made a big mistake that night. But we were two lonely people, and of all the gin joints in the world, we just happened to walk into the same one.'

'No, Sam!' she pleaded. 'Don't say that! What about love? Doesn't love count for anything?'

I took a long drag on the Marlboro.

'Oh, sure, precious. Maybe you loved me, and maybe I loved you. But you're going to do time. In bars. And discos. Maybe five, maybe ten years. And when it's over, maybe I'll be there, maybe I won't. But I'll always remember you.'

Standing there, she looked like she'd been kicked in the head by an entire line of tiller girls.

'But Rick – what about Paris?'

My name isn't Rick, angel. That must have been somebody else.'

Outside, the rain had turned to a monotonous staccato on the windowpane – kind of like Philip Glass on glass. I expected her to waltz out, but she rushed at me instead.

'You're such a fool, Sam,' she sobbed, beating her fists against my chest. 'Wake up and smell the cappuccino! You're still acting the way you did in *The Big Sleep*! Who cares that I slept with all those other people? Haven't you seen *The Big Chill*? Haven't you ever heard of the sexual revolution?'

A guy hates to let a future ex-girlfriend down hard, but I had to do it.

'The sexual revolution is over,' I told her, grinding out a Marlboro.

She tilted her head and looked at me through her baby-blue contacts.

'Really? Who won?'

'Nobody,' I said flatly. 'Nobody at all.'

For a moment, the two of us stared at each other like long lost lovers who had just run into each other at somebody else's wedding. Finally she turned and smiled.

'Well, Sam . . . do you want to do it anyway? Do you want to play it again, for old times' sake?'

I shook my head. 'You just don't get it, do you, precious?'

She didn't answer.

'Look, I'm no good at being noble, but it doesn't take much to see that casual sex only makes for casual enemies. We shouldn't have slept together that night, and we're not going to sleep together now.'

She bummed a Marlboro and sneered.

'You think you're a tough guy, don't you, Sam?'

'No, precious. A nice guy. And in 1987 nice guys – and nice girls – sleep alone.'

For a moment, she seemed a little confused. But she was a modern girl, and snapped back faster than the elastic on a £150 track suit. She ran a mousse through her hair and walked to the door.

'Well, Steve –'

'Sam.'

'Right. Well . . . if you ever want me, you know how to get me.'

I expected her to say something about putting my lips together and whistling, but she was too eighties for that.

'You can leave a message on my machine,' she said. 'After the beep. You know what the beep is, don't you, Steve?'

And she was gone. As I heard her Reeboks echo down the hall, I thought about our first – and only – date together. It was too bad it had to end this way; if we hadn't slept together, it might have been the start of a beautiful friendship. But of all the gin joints . . .

15

Oh, what the hell. I buzzed my secretary.

'Frank,' I said, lighting up a Marlboro. 'Get me the operator.'

'What for, Mister Spade?'

'I hear she's cute. Maybe she needs a date Saturday night.'

Yes, the sexual revolution is over.

The battle was fought on the beaches (Brighton, Blackpool), in the air (*Dynasty*, *Dr Ruth*), and even at sea (remember waterbeds?).

And after twenty-odd years of being able to have sex with anyone or anything on a first date . . . After twenty-odd years of 'long and meaningful relationships' that lasted somewhere between twelve and twenty-four hours. . . . And after twenty-odd years where some of us have put so many notches in the bed that the frames have turned to sawdust (not to mention the establishment of an entire fashion of dating known as the 'They come at night, they go at night' school of interpersonal relationships).

The pendulum has begun to swing back. Because what has finally crawled out of all those beds is a group of people who are sadder, but wiser. People who've learned the basic truth of sex – the one thing that never came up in all those late-night university discussions about 'doing it':

Sleeping with somebody changes everything.

One person inevitably wakes up the next morning hoping it's going to be more than 'just one night' while the other is looking for an ejection button on the side of the mattress and can't understand 'How did I go to bed with a date and wake up with a relationship?'

And today these people – these, for lack of a better word, 'nice guys' and 'nice girls' – have begun to ask the following questions:

– Do we really need to wake up in any more strange beds?

– Do we really need any more 'late greats' to avoid in restaurants?

– Are there really any positions we all haven't tried at least once?

And moreover:

– Are any of us really proud of the fact that if a job application called for character references, more than just a few of us could list the local sofa bed company.

Yes, these are sobering times.

All of which explains why, if the motto of the sixties and seventies was 'I'm okay, you're okay, so let's sleep together,' the watchwords of the eighties are slightly different: 'I'm okay, but I'm not too sure about you, so let's not. At least not yet.'

(I mean, come on. At this point haven't we all had enough of those awkward early morning conversations where somebody says 'I'll call' and then adds, 'It was nice to meet you. Would you mind closing the door on your way out?')

What follows in this book is a guide to dating during the eighties. A time when people are playing for keeps.

With luck, it may help you avoid some of the terminally deranged, the socially insane, or the emotionally crippled – those wonderful walking wounded who are incapable of sustaining a relationship past sunrise.

Or, with still more luck, it may prevent you from becoming one.

So if you're about to begin a relationship or are even vaguely attracted to someone, keep the following in mind.
– Get plenty of rest.
– Drink plenty of fluids.
– And don't operate heavy machinery.

Given the chance, Ernest Hemingway might have looked back at the sexual revolution and said 'It was good.'

But perhaps the more pertinent question is asked every night in millions of bedrooms all over the world.

'Was it good for you too?'

To which there is only one appropriate response:

'I'm tired, darling. Let's talk about it in the morning.'

How to Spot Nice Guys

- Nice guys still pick the woman up on a date.
- Nice guys still pick up the bill.
- Nice guys still believe in chivalry: In bed, it's only polite to make sure the woman comes first.

How to Spot Nice Girls

- Nice girls don't order lobster.
- A nice girl will never kill someone and blame it on PMS.
- Nice girls always offer to split the bill – and are invariably stunned when some jerk takes them up on it.
- And every nice girl keeps at least one set of toy handcuffs in her bedroom – and knows *exactly* what old school ties and mattress handles are best used for.

1

The Two Greatest Lies of Blind Dates

1) 'She's got a great personality.'

2) 'Stand him on his money, he gets taller.'

Dating in the
Difficult Eighties

The Eternal Question

'If I have one more bad date I'm going to commit ritual suicide on the sweets trolley. I mean why *do* we date? Why do we put ourselves through this ridiculous process?'

'How about love, happiness, and the search for everlasting bliss?'

This is 1987. Let's deal with reality.'

'All right, then children. *Somebody's* got to extend the species.'

'That isn't why we date. That's why we . . .'

'Okay, okay. I've got it. I know why we date.

'Why?'

'Despite all the angst and aggravation, it all comes down to one simple, basic, human need. It's an emotion as old as . . .'

'Enough already! What is it? Why do we date?'

'We all need somebody to have dinner with.'

2

Today's Date:
It's Not an Adventure,
It's a Job

'I met him at the candy store.
He turned around and smiled at me
– get the picture? (Yes, we see.)
That's how I fell for the Leader of the Pack.'
                                        – The Shangri-Las

Another decade, another date.

Somehow, it wasn't supposed to turn out like this.

Yet there you sit in another fern-filled restaurant, eating yet another chef's salad, listening to yet another stranger tell you their life story.

You feel like you're on emotional autopilot.

And as you smile in all the right places, trying to appear utterly fascinated by the way Herbalife forever changed your date's life –

Your mind begins to wander, questioning whether you really should have ordered that second Bloody Mary.

Or whether that big deal is going to come through at the office.

Or whether it just wouldn't have been easier to exchange CVs and skip the meal.

Which is just the moment when you realize that you've been out on enough dates in the past few years to fill the E–K section of the London telephone directory.

And not one of your friends is available to cut this one short by phoning in a bomb threat.

How did this happen to us?

How did we end up in the land of a thousand dates?

They say those who do not learn from the past are doomed to repeat it.

And unless you really like the idea of having your epitaph read 'I came, I saw, I dated' (or, for the more promiscuous among us, 'I saw, I dated, I came') perhaps it's worth a look back.

The Method of Modern Love: An Interview with Sigmund Freud

(Please note: Although Sigmund Freud has not given a public interview since his death in 1939, we contacted him last year through his agents in London and prevailed upon him to offer a few words to the readers of this book. The interview took place in the front seat of a white 1979 Jaguar on the Cromwell Road while the doctor was driving between an art auction and the January sale at Harrods. For the record, it should be noted that Freud wore a seat belt, smoked Marlboro Lights, and sang along with Kris Kristofferson's 'Me and Bobby McGee' on the radio.)

Dr Freud, where exactly did we go wrong?

The way I see it we've made three mistakes. First, we should have bought British Telecom shares. Second, I should have bid more for that Keith Haring canvas – collecting art is the next major boom industry for Yuppies. And third, I think we just missed the exit for Harrods.

Actually, I was talking about dating –

Are you *sure* that's what you want to discuss?

Yes.

Well . . . it's your forty-five minutes. Go ahead.

Okay. As a generation, where exactly did we go wrong? How did we get so screwed up?

Haven't you read my books? It's like anything else: you scratch the surface of a problem, you usually find sex underneath.

What do you mean?

Dating was never supposed to go on for fifteen years. It used to be

27

that you started dating in school, refined your technique at university, then grew up and got married so you could have sex. . . . But the sexual revolution changed all this: You no longer had to get married to have sex. . . . You no longer had to grow up and get married. . . . In fact, you no longer had to grow up at all. So dating – which was once the sport of teenagers – suddenly became something that could go on forever. Or, to paraphrase your Tom Wolfe – the sexual revolution allowed you to 'push the performance envelope of adolescence just about to its outer limits. . . .'

Wait a minute. You've actually read The Right Stuff?

Sure. It's an excellent example of male bonding. If we'd only had that symbolism in my day, back in Vienna, two guys on a rocket, blasting into space . . . The mind reels. . . .

Can we get back to dating?

It's your interview.

So what effect did all this have on us?

Like I said, dating was only supposed to be a short-term affair. But you kids have turned it into a second vocation. You're the first generation to date for almost two decades, and the problem is that you're no damn good at it. None of you knows the right way to act anymore. You're confused. And the rules . . . The rules seem to change faster than – what was the name of that kid who wore the white glove two years ago?

Michael Jackson?

Right. The rules seem to change faster than this month's pin-up in *Just 17* magazine. I mean – on a date – who pays? Who asks who out? Should the guy try to sleep with a woman on the first date? Should the woman be more offended if he does try, or if he doesn't? And as you get older, the problem becomes even more acute. You've been through so many relationships that you either try too hard or become overprotective. . . . You have so much emotional baggage. . . .

Forget about emotional baggage. This generation needs emotional transit vans.

Precisely. Eventually you get to the point where you've been through so much and you're so used to living alone that you don't have the slightest idea how to cope with somebody else.

I went out with a girl like that the other night. I told her I'd pick her up at eight o'clock, and there was a long silence on the line. Finally she said, *'You must be thin.' I had no idea what she was talking about until she revealed, 'I don't eat after six. I'm on a diet.'*

Exactly my point. All that time spent in solitary has made more than a few of you go stark raving mad. . . . But I suppose I shouldn't complain. It's been great for the psychiatry industry.

Do you . . .

Jesus! Did you see the bazooms on the chick in that GTI? Damn! They were breasticles! . . .

Can we get back to dating?

Has anyone ever told you that you're compulsive?

No.

You're compulsive.

Thanks. Getting back to dating, is the fact that we can date forever the only thing that's gone wrong?

No. Not at all. There are four and a half billion people in the world today. Correct?

I think so.

And there is no rush to get married, right?

Right.

So, what with discount airfares, lots of overseas business travel, and massive numbers of refugees trolling the high seas – the political policies of the Khmer Rouge resulting in 'boat people,' the tax policies of Margaret Thatcher resulting in 'yacht people' – it's easy to see how some of you have come to believe that there's always going to be somebody better coming around the corner. You think there's always going to be somebody funnier, somebody more attractive, or someone more intelligent than – as you put it – that person who's sitting across the table sipping the Bloody Mary eating that chef's salad. So no matter what, the poor soul is never going to be your dream date. . . . And those dinners go on endlessly.

But . . .

Wait. That's only half the problem. There's a second group of people who are even worse. They've become totally confused about the difference between people and property. . . . They've read too many Sanderson Wallpaper ads, and seen too many BMW commercials.

What do you mean?

We all want what we can't have. There are people who think that if something comes too easily, it can't be any good; or, turned about

29

for dating, if somebody likes us, they can't possibly be right. As Marx might have said –

Karl?

No. Groucho. Karl had a totally different set of problems. All public figures do. Hitler had an overbearing mother. Gaddafi wasn't properly toilet trained. And Joseph Stalin . . . Stalin was moody. He had mood swings that lasted forty years. . . . In any case, I call this problem the Groucho Marx doctrine of dating: 'I could never go out with anybody who'd want to go out with me.'

I was in love with somebody like that once.

Do you want to talk about it?

Sure . . . I met this woman who I loved more than anything in the world. She was smart, she was funny – and although my friends didn't think she was at all attractive, I looked at her with my heart instead of my eyes.

What do you think that means?

Love is not only blind, but also deaf, dumb, and stupid.

Go on.

Anyway, no matter what I did – love letters, flowers, even marriage proposals, the only time she was interested in me was when I wasn't interested in her.

Mmmm-hmmm.

Anyway, after enough times of being stood-up, and late-night heart-to-heart talks, I stopped calling her. At which point two weeks would pass, and she'd call me. She'd get on the phone in a small, cooing voice and say, 'Hi. I miss you. I love you, I need you and I care for you.' So I'd get all excited and reply, 'Great! You know I've always felt the same way. Let's get together!' And because she knew she had me back, she'd say, 'I'd love to, but I can't. I have dates every night this week.' Eventually it got to the point where I called her 'Miss Bhopal.' She had the personality of a Union Carbide plant – anybody got downwind, they died.

That's very interesting.

No. It's pathetic.

Do you still love her?

Of course.

If she walked through the door would you still marry her?

Of course.

You're right. It's pathetic. That'll be £75. Maybe you should consider coming in two or three times a week.

Is Dating the Cruellest Game?

Some people think dating is a game. They say you should play hard to get; they think you should always keep the other person guessing.

This is wrong.

You play football. You play the stock market. You do not play games with other people's hearts. (Yes, dating may be the second national pastime, but it's not an Olympics-sanctioned sport. There are no gold medals for doing swan dives onto somebody's head; nobody scores a perfect 10 by winning the 200-metre free-style heartbreak event.)

Essentially, there are two reasons to play games. One is to get somebody; the other is to string them along.

Let's consider both.

First off, if you play games to get somebody – standing people up, not answering the phone when you're really there, or inventing that phantom boyfriend or girlfriend – just where do you think this is going to get you?

Married?

Great. Then what? Now that you've played hard to get, what are you going to do for the rest of your life?

Play hard to keep?

Then there are people who play games to string someone along – the people who keep you around for company while they're out looking for somebody better.

(You know the type – the 'Oh, I forgot about your firm's party on Saturday night. I have to have dinner with my dying aunt,' who is actually a twenty-three-year-old aerobics instructor at the Pineapple Dance Studios.)

If you act like this, be forewarned:

God will get even with you.

He will steal your car radio, cancel your insurance, have your company bought out by Attila the Hun (thus relieving you of both your job *and* company car), and then jam every video you own.

And if this doesn't convince you to stop, He'll visit you with the modern-day equivalent of lice, boils, and plagues:

He'll make you fall in love with someone who plays the games even better than you do.

Very funny. I see we're almost out of time, so we should begin to wrap this up. Getting back to dating . . .

You really are obsessed with this. Don't you ever get out? Go to a film?

Dr Freud, would you say the sexual revolution was like a giant dinner party, with a thousand things to taste and sample, and now the time has come to pay the bill?

I wouldn't. But you can. Have you ever considered a career in advertising? Or the catering business? You seem to have some kind of strange fixation with food. Quiche is very close to kiss . . .

Returning to the problem at hand, how do we get out of those restaurants?

Ask for the bill.

You can do better than that. You're denying the problem.

Okay. First of all, you can start by avoiding the 'always something better coming around the corner' types, and the Miss Bhopals.

A Brief History of Dating, or Would Cleopatra and Mark Anthony Have Been Happier if They'd 'Defined the Terms of Their Relationship'?

Contrary to popular belief, Oedipus did not sleep with his mother, gouge his eyes out, and invent the blind date.

Dating is strictly a twentieth-century phenomenon. It exists mainly because the population grew too large and sophisticated for marriages to be arranged by our parents or matchmakers anymore. (Sorry, but there were no 'happy hours' at bars in medieval England.)

The important question, however, is: Did ancient people miss out on a great time by not dating?

That depends.

On one hand, the Marquis de Sade, Casanova, and Don Juan could probably have never adjusted to 'long and meaningful relationships'; Henry VIII was definitely not the kind of guy who'd sit down with one of his wives and say 'We have to talk'; and Mata Hari was certainly better off never having to explain that she 'wanted to see other people.'

But then there's Romeo and Juliet.

Who knows?

Maybe those two crazy kids would still be alive today if only one of them had asked:

'Just where is this going?'

How?

If you're going out with one – and they're easy to spot, as they're always looking over your shoulder at everyone else in the restaurant – just get up and walk out. And don't worry about being rude; they'll be too busy looking at everyone else in the room to even notice you're gone.

What about normal people? What's your advice for them?

Be kind to strangers.

What do you think that means?

We said there are four and a half billion people in the world, right? When you start seeing people, there are only six. Yes, *six*. And they all know each other. Word gets around fast. If you try to act somewhat 'of this earth' – meaning that you don't deliberately screw people up, lead anybody on, or act as if you're going on a search-and-destroy mission through life – even if the person who's sitting opposite you in that restaurant isn't right, maybe they'll know somebody who is. But on the other hand, if you insist on acting like, well, a Union Carbide plant, you'll be amazed at how fast the immediate world will be alerted.

That's very interesting.

I'm supposed to say that.

Do you want to go further?

You're stealing all my lines.

Mmmm-hmmm. Go on. I think we're getting somewhere.

Okay. The other thing you should do – if you really want to get out of those restaurants – is stop trying so hard. Stop all the panic. Stop reading all the psychological implications of when somebody rings or how they dress. You must remember this: A kiss is but a kiss. A sigh is but a sigh. Sometimes a date is just a date.

Well! I see we're out of time. But I think this has been a very fruitful session, and I think we've both learned something from it.

I agree. Shall we make another appointment?

Let me look in my book. How about next Tuesday at four?

Fine. I'll write you a cheque.

One last question . . .

What?

Why the January sale at Harrods?

You've got to be prepared. Nice people may sleep alone, but hopefully not forever.

You can do better than that.

Okay. Nice guys may sleep alone, but they *do* sleep at night. And when you consider the state of most people's affairs today, that's not so bad, is it?

3

A Thirty-second Trip to the Pictures: *Some Call It Sex*

Midnight. Fog blankets London. The only sound is the lone warble of a car burglar alarm – otherwise known as the mating call of the urban Porsche.

In a small English restaurant run by Sidney Greenstreet (played by John Candy), a young single man is murdered.

Gasps in the dining room. Shock in the kitchen. The blackened redfish turns green.

And since Kojak is busy on television, Charlie Chan appears out of the mist. Yes, the enigmatic Chinese detective, in John Travolta's white suit. Examining the corpse, Chan notices the victim has been shot through his address book. . . . And immediately deduces that the killer must have been one of the young man's former girlfriends.

More gasps in the restaurant.

Police cars roar out of headquarters.

Newspapers spin.

The suspects are rounded up at a central location and, as always, Chan announces, 'The murderer is in this room.'

But is the brilliant detective happy?

No.

Because in 1987 'this room' happens to be Leicester Square.

4

Better Relationships Through Technology

Q. What's the most important technological breakthrough in modern romance since the pill?

A. The telephone hold button. Because now it's possible to determine, scientifically, exactly where you stand with somebody. How?

If you click in on your girlfriend and she says 'Hold on. I'm on the phone with Daryl Hall, but I'll get rid of him,' you know everything's fine.

Or, if you're already on the phone with your boyfriend when his phone clicks and he says 'That must be Grace Jones again. She's driving me crazy, but I'll get rid of her,' you know your relationship is in good stead.

But the minute *you're* the one they're calling back, or the moment you start taking the other call – hang up. The romance is over.

Now admittedly you may want to 'reach out and punch someone.' But don't blame British Telecom. All they've done is saved you untold grief and aggravation. So look at it this way:

There are eight million numbers in the phone book.

You'll find another.

5

First Dates:
Travelling Into
The Heart of Darkness
in a Golf GTI

'We have a date with destiny.'

— Winston Churchill

*'Oh yeah? Well I hear Mike-ee's
got a date with some broad from
Manhattan. A college girl.'*

— The Godfather

*It's been seventeen years since Captain Willard (Martin Sheen) went up
the Nong River after Colonel Kurtz in* Apocalypse Now. *Following his
mission in Vietnam, Willard took part in the ill-fated 1980 Iranian rescue
attempt, received an honourable discharge, then returned to the United
States, where he purchased a sportswear franchise in a Californian
shopping centre.*

*As we pick up the story in 1987, Willard has just got out of bed in his
studio flat and is doing aerobics in front of a large mirror to* The Doors'
'The End.' A ceiling fan chops the air.

He accidentally smashes the mirror, and . . .

Single.

Shit.

It's Wednesday, and I'm still single.

When I was with somebody, I only wanted to be alone. And when
I was alone, I only wanted to be with somebody.

'You have to make friends with horror,' Kurtz told me in the jungle. 'Horror has a face, and a name.'

He was right.

Its name was Janice Greenblatt.

Its face was courtesy of Dr Stanley Schofield, Beverly Hills plastic surgeon.

The two of us didn't say a word for six months, until I finally said, 'Charlie don't surf. And Charlie certainly don't make commitments.'

That was a year ago.

And now I sit in this flat getting lonelier every day.

Getting softer.

Getting weaker.

While she's out there getting laid.

I needed more than a mission.

I needed a date.

I missed the action. I missed the adventure. I missed the sheer adrenaline of it.

Maybe it had something to do with 'Nam.

But maybe they explain it better in the MI5 Dating Manual:

Why There is Nothing More Terrifying Than a First Date:

No catastrophe, natural or man-made, is cumulatively more stressful. Consider the following:

- You don't have to dress nicely for a hijacking.
- You don't have to be on your best behaviour during an earthquake.
- You don't have to be funny and charming during a plane crash.
- You don't have to be punctual for a mugging.
  And let's face it:
- All of these things happen by surprise; nobody calls you up a week in advance and invites you out to an Apocalypse. Now do they?

Thursday, 9 December, 0900 hours. Willard meets the General (G.D. Spradlin) and his assistant, Jerry, at their local Macdonald's in downtown L.A.

Willard enters, salutes, and:

'Captain Willard, Special Forces, retired, reporting as requested.'

Jerry appeared from behind the deep fryer carrying my dossier and a Big Mac.

'Captain Willard,' he began, 'is it not true that in the spring of 1984 you once used to go out with Doreen Holden and never asked her out again because she used the word *we* sixty-one times during your first date? As in "We should make plans for Christmas." Or "We have to get tickets to see Madonna." Is it not true that at the end of the date you stood up and said, "I don't know about *we*, but *I'm* going home"?'

Yes it was true. You never learn to trust anybody who uses the word *we* too soon – unless it's to say 'We'll jump off that bridge when we come to it.' It's the same way you never trust anyone who refers to their old girlfriends or boyfriends as lovers – as in 'My last lover took me skiing in Gstaad.' These are people you don't want to be in the same country with, let alone the same bed.

I faced Jerry.

'No, sir. I have no knowledge of any such date with a Doreen Holden. . . . Nor, if such a date had taken place, would I be inclined to discuss it.'

The General moved over from the cash till 'I thought we might have a bite to eat before we talked, Willard.'

The three of us sat down at a large Formica table with an order of french fries. The General pulled out an eight-by-ten glossy of a pretty young woman and slid it across a grease slick to me.

'Have you ever heard the name Katherine Kurtz?'

'You mean Colonel Kurtz's daughter?'

The General bit his lower lip. 'She was a fine woman. Right school, university, London School of Economics. But sometimes, you get out there, playing the field . . . your dating methods become . . . unsound.'

'Unsound, sir?'

'Play him the tape, Jerry.'

He popped a cassette into a stolen BMW Blaupunkt. The machine whirred, and I heard a cheery, kind voice:

'Hi. I'm not here right now, but if you leave your name and number after the tone, I'll get back to you as soon as I can.'

So far she didn't sound particularly strange. I'm always suspicious of anybody whose answering machine messages are too twee; it's usually a sign of desperation – not unlike people who use *we* on first dates.

'This next tape,' the General said, 'was made during one of Miss Kurtz's last dates. I think you'll find it rather interesting.'

The machine whirred again. I heard the clink of wineglasses and the clatter of cutlery on china. Her voice was like nothing I'd ever heard before – she sounded eerie and detached, as if she were talking over a long-distance phone line on Valium.

'I see a married couple . . . walking along a white paling fence . . . with a baby buggy . . . in Stamford, Connecticut. This is my dream . . . this is my nightmare. . . .'

The General and I stared at each other, saying nothing.

Somehow, I couldn't match the face with the voice. She looked so sweet and innocent, and yet . . .

Why do people always put their worst foot forward on a date? Why do they always show their greatest insecurities?

Maybe it was nerves. Maybe it was 'Nam.

'I don't know why people act like that,' the General sighed. 'But we're worried about her, Willard.' He hesitated. 'It should be obvious that because of all the dating, all the pressure . . . Miss Kurtz has gone insane.'

Her voice echoed in my head? *'This is my dream . . . this is my nightmare.'*

'Yes. Obviously, sir. Quite insane.' I took a deep breath. 'What would you like me to do about it?'

The General shifted uneasily in his chair. Jerry handed me a chicken nugget. The pronouncement was swift and fast, falling on me like napalm from an F111.

'Take her out,' he said.

Shit.

We all knew what that meant:

Drinks after work.

If we liked each other, dinner.

I wanted a date and now I'd got one.

The only problem was which night to ask her out.

Friday night was the weekend. Too much pressure.

Saturday night is worse.

Sunday is homework night, Monday everybody's tired, and Thursday is too close to Friday.

But . . . shit.

Here it was Thursday, and I was still single.

It would have to be Friday night.

I took the date.

I took the chicken.

What the hell else was I going to do?

'Remember the one rule of all first dates, Willard,' the General warned me as I walked toward the door.

I had no idea what he was talking about.

'Somebody fixed you up, right?'

'Yes, sir.'

'All first dates are like being on *Dragnet*. Everything you say can and will be used against you.'

Outside, I fired up the GTI. As I drove away her voice still haunted me. I slipped 'Ride of the Valkyries' into the cassette deck and thought about another chapter in the CIA Dating Manual:

Friday. 10 December. 1900 hours (seven-ish, in civilian terms). Coming in low, out of the sun, Willard drives his GTI to Katherine Kurtz's flat in West Hollywood.

Not wanting to appear too anxious, Willard has circled the block a half dozen times to make sure he's seven minutes late. He gets out of the GTI carrying a bouquet of lilies, climbs the steps and:

'The horror. The horror.'

Kurtz's voice in the jungle kept coming back to me.

His daughter's voice on the phone was worse:

'Let's meet for lunch,' she said.

We both knew the game: Lunch is less dangerous than dinner. It's got a time limit. You can always cut it short by claiming you have to be back at the office – either to fix a nuclear reactor, clamp a few cars or have a meeting with Micky Duff.

'How about dinner?' I countered, trying to make light of it. 'I don't know about you, but I can't take a date seriously unless it starts after sunset.'

'Fair enough,' she laughed.

For a moment I debated asking where she wanted to eat.

I was going to ask out of courtesy.

Creating the Wrong Impression:
How to Make Sure Your First Date
Is Your Last Date

For Women:

1) Describe, in great detail, the problems with your ovaries, your diet, your thighs, and your mother.
2) Leave a copy of *Bride's* magazine on your coffee table.
3) Say things like 'I love Lamborghinis,' especially if your date is driving a Fiesta.
4) Put on your makeup at the table. (Yes, the natural look is in – tons of it.)
5) Sneer and complain if he holds a door open for you. (This is *always* an attractive way to let him know you're an independent woman.)
6) Describe everyone you've ever gone out with as being either crazy or insane. (Don't worry. Never in a million years will anybody begin to suspect that maybe your behaviour played a part in these matters.)
7) Slip your phone number to the waiter.

For Men:

1) Have your secretary ring and say you're going to be twenty minutes late. (It's always a wise idea to let her know just how important you are.)
2) Leave a copy of *Penthouse* on your coffee table.
3) Within five minutes of meeting, impress her by revealing exactly how much money you make. (Be subtle. Mention your Swiss Banking Account and tax hideaway in Guernsey.)
4) Casually mention that your last girlfriend was a model.
5) And that she appeared in *Vogue's* swimsuit issue.
6) And then remark 'But I'm not into looks anymore.'
7) Let her know how sensitive you are by complaining about how many strange beds you've woken up in lately.
8) Forget your wallet, be overdrawn on your credit cards, and announce 'You get this one. I'll get the next.'

I was going to ask because these are the eighties, and women should have equal say in how they spend their time.

But somehow these things always get turned around.

You come off as weak.

And indecisive.

And although nobody's masculinity should rise and fall on things like who chooses the restaurant or who makes the dinner reservations, I've learned one thing:

There are times when a guy should be the guy.

And this was one of them.

'We'll eat at Marty's,' I told her. It was a small place on Sunset Boulevard. Not too cheap, not too expensive. The last thing you want to do is take somebody to one of those seven-course expense-account extravaganzas with a fake French maître d', a menu that features things like 'braised ribs of baby baboon pizza *en croûte*,' and prices that could break a Swiss bank. There's already enough pressure on a first date; putting your life's savings on the table is only going to make the woman feel as though you expect some kind of tangible return on your investment at the end of the night.

'Marty's is great,' she said. 'I'll meet you there.'

'Negative,' I told her. This was another game we both understood – separate cars. Separate destinations when dinner was over. An easy way to avoid those awkward late-night scenes in front of somebody's house at midnight.

I have a better idea,' I told her. 'This is Los Angeles and there are only two of us. So why don't we take *three* cars? Or four?'

If a smirk can travel over the phone wires, hers did.

'You win,' she said.

'I'll pick you up at eight.'

That was yesterday.

And now I stand here, outside her door, ready to ring the bell.

The only problem is that it's 7:00.

And now I have to circle around the block for another hour.

Shit.

There are times when a guy should be the guy – and I wish this wasn't one of them.

But at least it gave me time to read another chapter in the CIA Dating Manual:

46

The Greatest Lies of First Dates

1) 'It happened a long time ago, and I'm over him.'
2) 'My flat never looks like this.'
3) 'She's your *daughter*? My God! I could have sworn you two were sisters!'
4) 'It's up to you. I don't care where we eat.'
5) 'I've never been here before.'
6) 'I don't usually act like this.'
7) 'Don't worry. Everybody mispronounces words in a French restaurant.'
8) 'You're not fat.'
9) 'No. Really. You look fine.'
10) 'I've never told this to anybody before.'
11) 'I never listen to my mother.'
12) 'Money doesn't mean that much to me.'
13) 'I'm 29. I skipped two years at school.'
14) 'Has anybody ever told you that you're beautiful?'
15) 'No. You're the first.'
16) 'I *really do* like sleeping alone.'
17) 'I'd love to stay over, but I have an important meeting in the morning.'
18) 'I had a great time.'
19) 'I'll call you.'
20) 'I never sleep with anybody on a first date.'
21) 'When I meet somebody, I'll stop smoking.'

Friday. 10 December. 2010 hours. Willard has cruised the neighbour-hood for an hour. In the interim he stopped at a 7–Eleven and accidentally spilled a Triple Shake on his tie as he browsed through the latest issues of Soldier of Fortune *and* The Economist. *Back on the street, he observed that every GTI – all twelve million of them – seemed to have personalized license plates (Willard's own read 'Z-Horror,' although his first choice was 'Apocalypso Man'). Finally, passing a restaurant with a car* *attendant service, he calculated that it costs him $20,000 a year to keep a car in Los Angeles – $4,000 in car payments and another $16,000 to buy it back from the parking attendants every night at two bucks a throw.*

The hour passed, Willard parks the car, takes the flowers, and moves to her door. He rings the bell, and:

'Coming!'

Shit.

It was now eight on Friday and I was still single.

I'd asked for a date, and I'd got one.

And now I was sure I wasn't dressed right.

I wasn't tall enough.

My trousers were too short.

My shoes were wrong.

My tie was stained.

And Lord only knew what kind of horror lurked on the other side of that door.

'Coming! I'll be there in a sec!'

I wanted to terminate the date right there and then – with extreme prejudice. But there was no turning back.

'It's nice to meet you,' she said, opening the door.

Somehow, she wasn't what I expected. She was tall, with wavy dark hair, baby-powder dimpled cheeks, hazel eyes, and the faintest of two beauty marks just in front of her left ear.

She was pretty.

And at the first glimpse of her, my worst suspicions were confirmed:

I wasn't dressed right. I wasn't tall enough. My trousers were too short. And I was going to burn those damn shoes as soon as I got home.

Exposing my tie, I handed her the flowers.

'These are so sweet,' she said.

'Chivalry isn't dead,' I joked. 'It's just been in a coma.'

She laughed and brought me into the living room with a wave of her hand. 'I'll be ready in a minute,' she said. 'Make yourself at home while I finish up in the bathroom.'

Had she noticed my tie?

I didn't think so.

Left alone, I began to survey the flat. No, there were no copies of *Bride's* magazine on the coffee table; the bookshelves were filled with real books, not just a Gombrich's *The Story of Art* left over from university and a Coppertone-stained edition of *Hollywood Wives*. There was even a copy of the *Spectator* on the end table. I took all of this as a good sign. It's always more interesting to spend time with someone who expresses a passing interest in the world around them; it gives you something to talk about while you're waiting for the car to be brought round.

'There's vodka in the fridge,' she called out.

I smiled, trying to avoid looking at my tie in the mirror. I started to contemplate some of the truly great mysteries of twentieth-century contemporary society:

– Why is it that you can give a woman six weeks' notice for a date, and she'll still only be putting on her makeup when you arrive at the door?

– Why is it that you can give a man a year's notice for a date, and he still won't begin to get dressed until it's six minutes before it's time to leave?

– Why can't I have money for nothing and chicks for free?

The minutes ticked by. I had time to think about two other chapters in the manual:

Why You Should Always Check Out Somebody's Flat on a First Date

It's called the furniture test.

There's almost nothing more important than seeing how somebody lives.

Is the flat still decorated like a student's room?

Are they still sitting on mum's hand-me-down sofa?

Are the records still tacked in blue plastic milk crates, and the bookshelves made of planks and bricks?

If this is the case, get out quickly.

Scram.

If somebody hasn't been able to grow up without you, the prognosis for making them grow up with you is not good.

And if your own place looks like this, keep one thing in mind: middle-aged adolescence is not an attractive sight.

And:

Never on a Sunday, or a Monday: The Pet Rule

Beware of anyone with animals. Cats, dogs, or zebras – the only thing worse than a person with a pet is somebody with two.

Why?

It has nothing to do with mankind's love of animals

A guy buys a dog because he thinks it'll help him pick up girls.

A woman buys a dog because it gives her an excuse to get home early.

In either case, you can't win.

If the relationship works, in three weeks you're going to be walking the animal in the middle of the night; and if the relationship fizzles, you're going to be home alone while they have a warm, loving animal who idolizes them to commiserate with.

Plus, there's one other thing.

In the short term, who needs to compete for somebody's affections with a canine?

'I'm ready,' she said, walking out of the bathroom.

She looked more than beautiful. She was stunning.

And thank God she wasn't wearing the perfume that always takes me back to darker days.

. . . Charlie.

Janice Greenblatt's perfume.

Katherine took my arm and we walked into the twilight.

The city lights twinkled.

The air was magnolia.

A helicopter hovered in the distance.

As I started the car I knew we were into the hardest part of the journey. I turned on the radio and thought about another chapter in the manual:

Read Between the Lines

On first dates, everyone speaks in tongues.

When somebody says 'I need time,' it usually means they need time to find somebody else.

If somebody says 'Go slow,' it usually means go away.

If a man says 'I can't get involved right now,' this generally means he isn't interested in getting involved with you. (I know it's painful, but we're all friends in this book, aren't we?)

If a guy says 'My wife and I are going through a trial separation,' this inevitably refers to a separation that will end in a trial.

And when a man says 'I really think two people should get to know each other before they sleep together,' this usually means: a) he hopes three and a half hours at dinner is enough time to get to know each other, b) he's going to try to sleep with you at the end of the date, and c) you'll never hear from him again if you don't.

Then there are the code words for women – usually used in reference to an old boyfriend:

'We date.' I sleep with John occasionally.

'We have an understanding.' I want to sleep with John all the time, but he wants to fool around.

'We're about to break up.' John and I still sleep together, and I'm out testing the waters – but I'll probably sleep with you just to make John jealous.

'I'm best friends with my ex.' John and I still sleep together when we're randy.

Friday. 10 December. 2200 hours (10:00 civilian time). Katherine and Willard are finishing their first bottle of wine. They both avoided ordering anything with garlic or onions – although Willard did stare in disbelief as the waiter announced the day's special was 'braised ribs of baby baboon pizza en croûte.' At the next table Francis Coppola has arrived and is having dinner with Robert Duvall. There's a flicker of recognition – but, no . . . it couldn't be. The waiter brings another bottle of wine, and:

'I hate dating.'

'No. *I* hate dating.'

'I hate dating more than you do.'

'Nobody could hate dating more than I do.'

'I hate dating more than anything in the *world*.'

'I'd rather have root canal than go on a date.'

The date was going wonderfully.

We'd hit it right off.

The food was perfect. The wine vintage. Neither of us started making plans to spend Christmas together in Khartoum; she didn't notice the stain on my tie until I pointed it out to her.

'I'm sorry I sounded so crazy on the phone,' she said. 'It's just that I've been out on so many dates . . .' She ran her finger around the edge of the wine glass, groping for the words. 'I think the biggest problem is trying to come to terms with the *Ms* Ethic we learned in the seventies and the *Mrs* Ethic that our mothers taught us when we were growing up. If you're too strong and independent, it scares guys off, and if you play it the other way, they think you're too needy.' She drank from her glass. 'I suppose it all comes down to one question: do you want the house with the white paling fence in Connecticut or the big office on Wall Street?'

I looked at her through the candles. 'Is that your dream or your nightmare?'

She lowered her eyes to the tablecloth. 'There's a conflict in every female heart,' she said. 'Between good and evil, a company directorship and children . . .' She stared out the window. 'And good does not always win. They say you can have it all, but nobody told us how to do it.'

I sympathized with her. 'The basic problem is that anybody born after 1945 is screwed,' I said, and she laughed.

'What's your dream and nightmare?'

I put my fork down. 'I picture a massive French restaurant. The size of an aircraft carrier. I walk in with a girl, and the maître d' looks at me, looks at a thousand empty tables, and says "I'm sorry but there's a forty-minute wait."'

'Would you like coffee?' the waiter asked.

'Yes please, thank you,' she said, and then excused herself. 'I'll be right back. I have to go to the ladies' room.'

As she walked away I couldn't quite remember the chapter in the CIA manual that explained why women habitually visit restaurant bathooms in twos – although I did recall something that went 'Cover me while I make a break for the stalls. . . .' But at that moment, I had another chapter on my mind:

The Waiter Rule

As you sit down to your first dinner together, observe carefully how your date treats the waiter.

Does he or she sneer 'Get me this, bring me that?'

Do they wince at the way the waiter places dishes on the table and nitpick unimportant details?

Do they treat the waiter like a slave?

And when the bill comes are they immediately distrustful, questioning every item?

Yes, keep a very close eye on the way someone treats the waiter on the first date.

Because this is exactly the way they're going to be treating you in six months.

'Your bill, sir.'

She reached across the table for it, but I got there first.

I took the bill.

I took her hand.

'I'll take you home,' I told her, and the two of us walked into the balmy blackness.

'What a beautiful evening,' she said, pulling close.

Yes, I thought. It reminded me of what Saigon might have been like – if only we'd won.

I thought about the last, and final, chapter in the CIA manual:

How to Tell if There's a Chance for a Relationship

- You're not upset about missing *Miami Vice*.
- You both love the way Springsteen sings about the working class but think there's something a little strange about people who go to his concerts in limousines.
- Your shoes seem to fit better.
- You ordered chicken but don't realize until halfway through the meal that you're eating veal.
- Instead of thinking about 'getting laid' you start thinking about 'making love.'

Saturday. 11 December. 0130-ish. In the cool, inky blackness of post-midnight Los Angeles, Willard quietly slips the GTI onto the freeway, easing into the darkened stream of asphalt, letting the current pull him along as he drifts into the night.

As his date and the lights of West Hollywood slowly recede behind him, he turns down his radio, and:

Saturday.

Shit.

It's Saturday, and I'm still single.

But then, maybe not.

Before I went on the date, I only wanted it to be over. And now that it's over, I only wish it had never ended.

She was not insane.

I was crazy.

'I hope I can see you again,' I said in the pale yellow light outside her door.

'That would be nice,' she sighed, and I looked in her eyes.

She was the kind of girl who loved the smell of Old Spice in the morning.

I kissed her softly on the cheek, and I walked down the stairs and started my car.

And now, as I drive home on the motorway, our final words keep coming back:

'Someday this dating is going to be over,' I told her.

Yes.

Someday this dating is going to be over.

6

The Clothing Rule

Occasionally someone comes along who offers to 'redecorate' you.

The woman, for example, who says 'Don't get me wrong. I think your Savile Row suits are perfect, but with just a few changes I could make you look like the lead guitarist in Sigue Sigue Sputnik.

Or the guy who thinks he's Bo Derek's husband and, after much soul-searching, opines 'Don't get me wrong. I think you're perfect, but you'd probably get even further up the ladder at Shell if you cut your hair, bleached it, wore less makeup, and dressed like Tina Turner.'

What these people really want is somebody else.

And if you give them an inch in a hemline, or two inches in the lapels, they'll not only change your shoes, socks, and trousers, but sooner or later they'll get around to your friends, your flat, your car, and finally your investment banking strategy.

And you still won't be the person they want.

But you will look like a fashion disaster.

In the end there's only one way to deal with these people.

At their first suggestion of change, simply say 'I think that's a great idea. But I think we should start by redecorating my flat.'

'How?' they'll ask.

'Leave.'

7

The Great
Unsolved Mystery
of Our Time

In the same night, in the same city, Craig and Barbara both go out on first dates.

Both of them go to nice restaurants.

Both of them see box office smashes.

And afterward they both take their respective dates home and screw their brains out.

The next morning, however, Craig and Barbara both wake up, look at who they've slept with, and decide they've made a terrible mistake and are never going to see the other person again.

Both their dates are heartbroken.

Why is it, then, that when Barbara tells us she'd had a one-night stand and has no regrets because 'It just didn't work out,' we're understanding and think she's a modern, adventurous woman?

And yet when Craig tells us the *same exact story*, our sympathy immediately goes out to the poor girl and we think he's a cruel, heartless bastard?

8

Male Dating Styles Through The Ages

	17	25	35	48	66
Drink	beer	whiskey	vodka	double vodka	Maalox
Seduction line	'My parents are away for the weekend.'	'My flatmate is away for the weekend.'	'My girlfriend is away for the weekend.'	'My wife is away for the weekend.'	'My second wife is dead.'
Enticement	'Want to see my new BMW?'	'Want to see my new flat?'	'Want to see my new house?'	'Want to see my new weekend house?'	'Want to see my son's BMW?'
Complaint	'My parents don't understand me.'	'My boss doesn't understand me.'	'My wife doesn't understand me.'	'My employees don't understand me.'	'My kids don't understand me.'
Favourite sport	sex	sex	sex	sex	sex
Drug	pot	coke	really good coke	power	coke, a Rolls Royce, the company jet
Definition of a successful date	'Tongue.'	'Breakfast.'	'She didn't set back my therapy'.	'I didn't bump into her kids.'	got home alive
Person he's most likely to have an affair with	his girlfriend's best friend	his girlfriend's flatmate	his wife's best friend	his secretary	his second wife's best friend
Favourite fantasy	geting to third	aeroplane sex	*ménage a trois*	floating his company	Swiss maid/Nazi sex slave

	17	25	35	48	66
House pet	roaches	stoned college flatmate	Irish setter	children from his first marriage	Fiona Richmond
Worst reason for not having sex	'My coach says not before a big game.'	'Big presentation at the office.'	'We did it last week.'	'My back hurts.'	'It reminds me of my last wife.'
Least believable lie	'She's only 17!'	'She's only 17!'	'She's only 17!'	'She's only 17!'	'She's only 17!'
Reason they can't make a commitment	'Haven't lived enough.'	'I'm waiting for my next rise.'	'I'm waiting for my next promotion.'	'I'm waiting for my next divorce.'	'I still haven't lived enough.'
Is it true that women fall faster but men fall harder?	'I'll never get over her.'	'I'll never get over her.'	'I'll never get over her.'	'I'll never get over her.'	'I think I'm finally over her.'
What's the ideal age to get married?	25	35	48	66	17
Worst sexual cliché	'You can't leave me like this.'	'But I *do* love you.'	'But it's *not* just one night.'	'But we do *like* each other.'	'But I'm *happy* it was good for you. Now what about me?'
Ideal date	Triple Stephen King feature.	'Split the bill before we go back to my flat.'	'Just come over.'	'Just come over and cook.'	sex in the company jet

9

Female Dating Styles Through The Ages

	17	25	35	48	66
Drinking alone	Diet Pepsi	Diet Pepsi	Diet Pepsi	Diet Pepsi	Pepsi
Drinking on a date	beer	black velvet	Diet Pepsi	champagne	whiskey sour
What's the idea age to get married?	28	28	28	28	28
Favourite drug	downers	coke and downers	coke, downers, and a corner office	really good coke, downers, a corner office, and Valium	affection
Least believable lie	'He's just somebody I study with.'	'He's just somebody I work with.'	'He's only a friend.'	'He's gay.'	'How could you say that? He was my best friend's husband!'
Second least believable lie	'He's more than an outside right.'	'He's more than a health-club instructor.'	'He's not a model, he's an actor.'	'How can you say that? He's my friend's son!'	'Professional jockeys happen to be very intelligent.'
Favourite sport	losing her virginity	shopping	tennis	watching her friends' marriages break up	sex
Battle cry	'Let's go steady.'	'I've got time.'	'I'm running out of time.'	'Gloria Steinem is still single.'	'So is Katherine Hepburn.'

	17	25	35	48	66
Most likely to have an affair with	her brother's best friend	her father's best friend	her husband's best friend	her son's best friend	the vicar
What she's really looking for	Mr Right	Mr Close	Mr Distinct Possibility	Mr Smith	the vicar
Stupidest line heard from a man	'You'd do it if you loved me.'	'You'd do it if you liked me.'	'It's better than sleeping alone.'	'At this point who's counting?'	'Wake me if you change your mind.'
Favourite complaint	'Men are crazy.'	'Men are crazy.'	'Men are crazy.'	'Men are crazy.'	'Men are crazy.'
Sexual fantasy	Billy Idol	on a 747 with her boyfriend – or Don Johnson	her boyfriend *and* Don Johnson	Don Johnson, her best girl-friend, her boyfriend, and Robert Wagner	Jethro from *The Archers*
Typical statement	'My mother thinks we're getting too serious.'	'My mother wants to know when we're getting married.'	'My mother won't even discuss it.'	'My daughter thinks we're getting too serious.'	'My grand-daughter wants to know when we're getting married.'
Most frustrating line to hear from a man	'I don't dance.'	'I always watch football on Sundays.'	'I'm too old for rock concerts.'	'I always do it this way.'	'What?'
Worst reason for not having sex	'It'll wake my parents.'	'It'll wake my flatmate.'	'It'll wake the neighbours.'	'It'll wake the kids.'	'You always fall asleep in the middle.'
Dream date	a weekend in London	a weekend in Paris	A weekend in Rio	a weekend with somebody else	a weekend anywhere but Bournemouth

10

Why a Divorced
36-year-old
Is a Better Prospect
Than a Single
36-year-old

After all those years on the open range, anybody who hasn't been married or hasn't had at least one long-term serious relationship by the time they're thirty-six isn't going to adjust too well to domestic captivity.

A thirty-six-year-old who's been divorced, on the other hand, has at least one thing going for her (or him): At one point they *tried* to make a commitment – and they probably have a pretty good idea of what went wrong and how not to make the same mistake twice.

Moving from the open range to more domestic metaphors:

First marriages today are like warm-up volleys at a tennis match.

They just don't count.

11

Updated Literature for the Eighties

Love Story: Does love still mean 'never having to say you're sorry'? Not a chance. As anyone who's been in a relationship lately will testify, love today is a constant, unending stream of apologies. In the '87 version, Jenny still gets cancer, but Oliver isn't all that heartbroken about it because it happens on the second date.

Portnoy's Complaint: The liver is relaced by tofu. He still complains. Only more so.

The Old Man and the Sea: An aging drug dealer smuggles cocaine back to Miami in a cigarette boat. The only problem is that he snorts most of it along the way. An eighties *Miami Vice* morality tale. In a rare cameo appearance, Edward Olmos says, 'Sink him.'

West Side Story: Recast as *Upper West Side Story*. The Jets (short for jet-setters) fight the Sharks (short for estate agents) in an intense battle for housing rights on Manhattan's Upper West Side. Officer Krupke is a woman. In the middle of the climactic fight scene, Maria complains that neither Tony nor Bernardo will treat her as an independent, intelligent woman. Upon hearing this, both men throw down their weapons in disgust and go off to commiserate at a local bar over Kir Royales.

The Great Gatsby: Re-released as *Interiors visits the Homes of West Egg*, Gatsby is now a corporate raider who slept with Daisy at Woodstock; Tom Buchanan is a has-been rock 'n' roller who was once in 'Bachman Turner Overdrive.' After appearing in *The Tatler* and having his parties covered by 'Bystander', Gatsby dies tragically during an interview for *Lifestyles of the Rich and Famous* when Robin Leach accidentally drops a camera in the Jacuzzi. Nobody comes to the funeral and Nick Carraway is sentenced by a High Court Judge for insider trading.

Gone With the Wind: Rhett still doesn't give a damn. But it's okay now, because Scarlett has a career.

The Scarlet Letter: A Ralph Lauren woman in Larchmont, New York, is caught having an affair with the local minister. Her husband divorces her, and she's forced to wear chain-store clothing for the rest of her life.

The Sun Also Rises: Nicaragua, 1987. Jake still doesn't sleep with Brett. 'We could have had such a damned good time together,' Brett says at the end of the book. 'Yes,' Jake replies. 'Isn't it trendy to think so?'

12

The Field Spotter's Guide to Dating Classifications

STUNT DATING

Age Group: 18+

General description: These are people who've just broken up with somebody (or have recently got divorced) and are out playing the field – with a vengeance. Occasionally known as 'rebounders,' or 'players,' this practice is sometimes also known as 'kamikaze dating.'

Modus operandi: Female: Expects to be taken to an expensive restaurant; she'll have a second date lined up for later that night after she kisses you good-bye on the cheek at her front door. Male: He'll go out with anybody, and sleep with anybody. Once.

Most likely to be met at: local bars, health clubs, art exhibitions, museum openings, group therapy sessions or the delicatessan. (Pickup line: 'It's so hard to cook a good meal for one.') The female is also likely to be met returning her engagement presents at Harvey Nichols.

Odds of starting a relationship with one: Zilch.

Current quotes: 'I recently broke up with this guy, and I just want to go out and have a good time. . . .' *And:* 'I'm not the marrying type.'

Quote three years from now: 'Jesus. I made a terrible mistake. Are you really sure you want to marry that guy?'

Short-term prognosis: Heartbreakers.

Long-term prognosis: Heartbroken.

AUCTION DATING

Age: 23+

General description: Also known as 'Sotheby dating,' these are people who are always holding out for a better offer. In the meantime they'll use you as 'backup' while they look around for something more interesting to do.

Modus operandi: This phone call is typical:

> You: 'Hi! What are you doing Friday night?'
>
> Them: 'I'm not sure yet. What about you?'
>
> You: 'I was wondering if you'd like to have dinner.'
>
> Them: 'I'd love to, but I can't. Somebody already invited me to a Sting concert.'

Odds of starting a relationship with one: Great, if you're Sting and your records are still selling. Otherwise it depends on how good your offer is.

Most likely to be met at: A party someone else has taken them to.

Comment: Don't feel too bad for them. As we all know, the best-laid plans of mice and social climbers usually fall through – and more often than not these people end up sitting home alone doing nothing.

Long-term prognosis: If you're a divorce lawyer, buy the summer house. The future of your practice is assured.

THE WALKING WOUNDED
(STAGE ONE)

Age: 28+

General description: Heart-on-the-sleeve time. These are people who've been through a series of tragic affairs, perhaps even a divorce. They have the uncanny ability to continually fall in love with the wrong person and never learn from the experience or get over them. Physically, there's lots of blinking back tears – which they'll explain as 'new contacts' until they get to know you better. Say, after five minutes.

Modus operandi: Vodka before dinner, vodka with dinner, vodka after dinner. They'll pour their hearts out, spending six hours telling you how badly their last girlfriend (or boyfriend) treated them – and then, as the air slowly disappears from the room, they'll announce 'But that's all in the past. Do you want to go to bed?'

Odds of starting a relationship with one: Great, as long as you're totally wrong for them.

Most likely to be met at: A blind date, a school reunion, or the credit department of a large department store where they're trying to explain why they've been too depressed to pay their bills for the past six months.

Favourite colour: Blue. Or black. Or black and blue.

Favourite film: What else? *The Way We Were.*

Ideal date: Suicide pact.

Comment: In truth, they really are warm, compassionate, romantic people; they're genuinely earnest when they say 'I just want to meet somebody and settle down.' But dating somebody like this is like being on the phone with British Telecom: 'All the lines are busy right now. Why don't you hang up and try to call again later?'

THE WALKING WOUNDED
(STAGE TWO)

Age: 32+

General description: By now they've been through too many heartbreaking romances and tortuous affairs. A certain Siberian bitterness has set in.

Modus operandi: You're sitting in a restaurant together. The waiter asks 'Blue cheese, thousand island, or Italian?' You pause, thinking, then answer 'Blue cheese.' At which point he (or she) stands and screams *'Goddamnit, you're all alike!'* then storms off.

Quote: 'I've had a vasectomy of the heart.'

Other quotes: (Male) 'I don't serve breakfast anymore.' (Female) 'Policemen are my friends.'

How they describe dating: Let's book *another* trip on the Titanic!

Most likely to be met at: 7–Elevens; the frozen-food section of any supermarket after 5 P.M.; the Betty Ford Clinic.

Odds of starting a relationship with one: Are you joking?

Advice: Wear bulletproof clothing. And let them order first.

POWER DATING

Age: 25+

General description: CV romance. These are women (and men) who think they can climb the business – or social – ladder on their backs (or whatever sexual position they happen to have a predilection for).

Modus operandi: They'll go out with you as long as it'll do them some good. They subscribe to something called 'The Stockmarket Dating Index' – meaning that when your stock drops, you're dropped.

Role models (in theory): Margaret and Denis Thatcher.

Role models (in reality): Faye Dunaway in *Network*, Evita Perón in Argentina; Imclda Marcos (while she was in power, buying shoes); John DeLorean; any plastic surgeon who's married a Hollywood starlet in the past few years; or any one of the lesser lights who've recently dated Elizabeth Taylor.

Odds of starting a relationship with one: It depends on who you can introduce them to, and what kind of business or social contacts you have to offer.

Chance for marriage: They don't marry. They merge.

Likelihood of divorce: They don't divorce. They divest.

Nightmare: Imelda and Ferdinand Marcos. (He dropped out of politics and she never had enough shoes.)

Other nightmare: A green American Express Card.

Most likely to be met at: Corfu at Christmas; any executive training seminar at the London Business School; Cannons Health and Fitness club; under the Chief Executive's desk. (Yes, men too.)

SUDDEN-DEATH DATING

Age: 32+

General description: The game is in overtime. After spending their twenties in a series of 'holding pattern' relationships, these people suddenly realize time is running out – it's time to get serious and get married. The women begin to say things like 'I'm on the verge of a biological meltdown.' The men suddenly wake up one day and realize that 'every night I go to bed with a strange woman is another morning I won't wake up to see my grandchildren.'

Motto: 'No more two-year relationships. The next one is it.'

Modus operandi: If it's not going to work – if there's no chance for marriage – they end it as quickly as possible. At the front door on a blind date if possible.

Most likely to be met at: College reunions, resident's association meetings, charity balls, opticians or in a car salesroom picking up their new Saab.

Odds of starting a relationship with one: Excellent.

Odds of ending a relationship with one: Forget it. You'd stand a better chance of getting out of Beirut International Airport alive in an El Al 747.

Favourite observation: 'It's amazing how much better off you are with a joint deduction.'

Quote, male: 'We'll register the kid for nursery school as soon as we get back from the honeymoon.'

Quote, female: 'Am I worried about taking his last name? Forget it. At this point, I'll take his *first* name too.'

Comment: Be kind to these people. Be understanding. If you play the field too long, you may end up being one.

13

Pre-relationship Agreements: An Idea Whose Time Has Come?

The woman was nervous as she unbolted the last of seventeen security locks on the front door of her flat.

'Hi,' she said, opening the door slightly. 'You must be David.'

The man in the hallway smiled. 'And you must be Lisa.'

'It's nice to meet you,' she said, opening the door still wider as she motioned to a woman standing just behind her in a business suit. 'This is my lawyer, Suzanne Hepplethwaite.'

'And this is mine,' David replied, yanking an Oxford man out of the shadows. 'Philip Nylon-DuPont.'

The lawyers shook hands.

'Well,' Lisa exclaimed. 'Now that we've all met, why don't you come inside? We might as well get to know each other while the lawyers work out our pre-relationship agreement.'

Pre-relationship agreements?

Absurd, you say?

Foolish?

The end of romance as we now know it?

Absolutely not. Think about it: We have pre-nuptial agreements between people who are in love. Separation agreements between people who are in hate. What could make more sense than a legally binding contract between perfect strangers? What could be saner than an agreement that sets down all the acceptable modes of behaviour before trouble can even begin?

With this in mind, the prestigious law firm of Punchem, Beatem, and Deckem has drawn up a sample pre-relationship agreement exclusively for the readers of this book.

Pre-Relationship Agreement

The party of the first part (herein referred to as 'he'), being of sound mind and fairly good body, agrees to the following with the party of the second part (herein referred to as 'she'):

1) *Full Disclosure:* At the commencement of said relationship (colloquially referred to as the 'first date' or 'blind date'), each party agrees to fully disclose any current marriages, dependent children, bizarre religious beliefs, phobias, fears, social diseases, strange political affiliations, or currently active relationships with anyone else that have not yet been terminated. Further, each party agrees to make known any deep-seated mother/father/sister/brother complexes and fanatical obsessions with pets, careers, or organized sports. Failure to make these disclosures will result in the immediate termination of said relationship before it has a chance to 'get anywhere.'

2) *Indemnification of Friends:* Both parties agree to hold the person who arranged the liaison (colloquially referred to as the 'matchmaker') blameless in the event the 'blind date' turns out to be a 'real loser.' (For the definition of a 'real loser' see *John DeLorean: My Story*, available at local bookshops.)

3) *Definition of Relationship:* Should said relationship proceed past first 'blind date', both parties mutually agree to use the following terminology in describing their said 'dating'. For the first thirty (30) days both parties consent to say they are 'going out.' (This neither implies nor states any guarantee of exclusivity.) Following the first thirty (30) days said parties may say they are 'seeing somebody' and may be referred to by third parties as 'an item.' Sixty (60) days following the commencement of 'first date' either member may elect to use the term 'boyfriend' or 'girlfriend' and their mutual acquaintances may refer to them as 'a couple.' Under no circumstances are the phrases 'my old lady,' 'my better half,' 'the little lady,' or 'my old man' acceptable. Further, if both members of the party consent, this timetable may be speeded up; however, if either

party 'gets too serious' and disregards this schedule, the other party may dissolve the relationship on the grounds of 'moving too fast' and may once again be said to be 'on the market.'

4) *Terms of Exclusivity:* For the first thirty (30) days both parties agree not to ask questions about the other's whereabouts at weekends, weeknights, or over long holiday periods. No unreasonable demands or expectations will be made; both parties agree they have no 'rights' on the other's time. Following the first six weeks or forty-five (45) days, if one party continues to be 'missing in action' without explanation, the 'wounded party' agrees to 'give up.'

5) *Dating Etiquette:* For the first thirty (30) days both members of the couple agree to be overtly considerate of the other's work pressures, schedules, and business ambitions. A minimum of three (3) phone calls will be made between the two parties during the working day, and each party will attempt – with best efforts – to originate 50 percent of the calls. Additionally, for the first two weeks all dates will be made at least twenty-four (24) hours in advance; there will be no 'running off in the middle of the night' to console an 'old boyfriend' and both parties agree to strike the phrase 'But he/ she *needs* me' from their vocabularies. Further, during the first six weeks each member of said relationship agrees to attempt at least one spontaneous 'home-cooked meal' and will arrange the delivery of at least one unexpected bouquet of flowers. Following the first forty-five days, both parties will return to their normal personalities.

6) *Terms of Payment:* It is agreed that – respective gross income aside – 'he' will pick up the bill at all dinners, discos, theatres, and breakfasts until (a) he considers her suitably impressed, (b) he is broke, or (c) she says, 'This is ridiculous – let's split it.' (Not included in this agreement are meals ordered in from the bedroom, which are subject to the availability of discretionary funds on hand at the time.)

7) *Living Arrangements* (occasionally known as the 'Why do I bother to keep my own apartment?' codicil): Should said relationship progress to the point where the couple spends more than five nights a week together, every effort shall be made to split the time evenly between their resective homes. Further it is agreed both sides will attempt to silence the lewd remarks of landlords or flatmates. Additionally, she will avoid having her mother call at 7:30 in the morning, and he agrees to remove traces of himself while in

residence at her flat, including washing his hairs out of the sink. (By the same token, she agrees to respect his right to keep his flat 'a mess.')

8) *The 90-Day Grace Period*: For the first three months each member of the couple agrees to hold the other blameless in the euphoric use of phrases like 'Let's move in together,' 'Why don't we start a family?' and – using archaic terminology – 'Let's get married.' Additionally, each party agrees to love, cherish, honour, and defend the other party's right not to meet his or her parents.

9) *The 'L' Word*: For the first sixty days both parties agree *never* to use the phrase 'I love you.' They may love plants, dogs, cars, concerts, or the way a particular pair of jeans fits, but *not each other*. Failure by one party to abide by this rule will result in the other party using the 'G' word: 'Gone.'

10) *Grounds for termination*: Any of the following will be considered just cause for the immediate and final dissolution of said relationship: (a) Excessive use of chatty French phrases; (b) ending any argument with the sentence 'My former wife/husband/girlfriend used to do the same thing'; (c) suggesting – no matter how kindly – that the opposite member should seek 'help'; (d) ending any argument with the phrase 'My analyst thinks you are . . .'; and (e) complaining more than twice about the contents of the other party's refrigerator. (Or lack thereof.)

11) *Declaration of Strength*: At the breakup each party reserves the right to make the other feel guilty by using one or all of the following phrases: (a) 'You'll never find anybody better'; (b) 'Nobody could ever make you happy'; (c) 'I'll find somebody who can really appreciate me'; and (d) My analyst thinks you are ——' (Psychosis to be filled in at the appropriate time.)

12) *Miscellaneous*: Each party agrees to give the other at least five minutes' notice before terminating said relationship; (b) both parties agree to remain exclusive until such time as the relationship appears to be 'on the rocks'; (c) at the termination of said affair, (1) both parties agree to be mature and return the compiled socks, sweaters, books, record albums, door keys, personal undergarments with all due haste through an impartial intermediary; (2) each party agrees to wait at least seventy-two (72) hours before engaging in sex with any of the other party's friends; (3) both parties agree to refrain from slandering the other for a period of at least seven days (bedroom

performance included), and further consent to use one of the following nebulous terms in describing the breakup: 'The timing wasn't right'; 'He/she wasn't ready for something serious'; 'He/she wanted more than I could give'; 'He/she was too involved in his/her career'; 'He/she decided to go back to his/her (a) spouse, (b) last lover, (c) hometown, (d) therapist.

13) *Addendum*: After the initial break-up – no matter what – both parties agree to 'give it at least one more shot.'

14

Another Trip to the Pictures: *The Pyjama Game*, 1987

Fade in:

INTERIOR: 30-YEAR-OLD MAN'S BEDROOM; NIGHT

We come in on a dishevelled room, lit only by the green glow of a stereo. A record spins idly on a turntable, the arm clicking in its final grooves.

Moving across the room, a blouse is strewn on the floor; also jeans, a man's shirt, and a bag and bra. A skirt is draped across a rowing machine.

On the night table, next to a bottle of wine, an ashtray overflows with cigarettes; a joint glows dull orange, about to go out. The digital clock reads 2:45 AM.

In the bed, a young man and woman lie naked under the sheets.

                    WOMAN
    ... That was nice.

MAN

Mmmm.

He turns on his back. She snuggles close.

WOMAN

Tired?

MAN

Exhausted ... You?

WOMAN

Blitzed.

(a quick kiss on his cheek)
Good night, Gary.

GARY

G'night.

She closes her eyes and drifts off to sleep.

CLOSE UP: DIGITAL CLOCK

3:05 AM. Twenty-five minutes have passed.

THE BED

The woman is fast asleep, but Gary is staring at the
ceiling. Something is gnawing at him, making him
nervous. Trying to dismiss it, he shuts his eyes and tries
falling asleep again.

CLOSE UP: DIGITAL CLOCK

3:30 AM. Another 25 minutes have passed.

THE BED

Gary still can't sleep. He's anxious. Edgy. He disen-
tangles himself from the woman and gets out of bed,
groping on the floor for something. He stubs his foot on
the rowing machine.

                    GARY

    Shit.

                    WOMAN

    Are you all right?

                    GARY
                (whispered)
    Yeah. Sure. Go back to sleep.

Finding what he's looking for, he goes to the bathroom,
turns on the light, and closes the door behind him.

INTERIOR: BATHROOM; NIGHT

Standing in front of the sink, he rifles the woman's bag.
He pulls out a diaphragm case, a makeup kit, her car
keys — but he isn't satisfied.

He goes through her wallet; cash, snapshots,
dry-cleaning receipts ... and finally finds what he's
looking for:

Her **driver's license**. He holds it up to the light. **Relief**. He
memorizes her name.

INTERIOR: BEDROOM; NIGHT

Switching off the bathroom light, he re-enters the room,
gets back in bed, and cradles the girl in his arms.

WOMAN
(sleepily)

...Are you okay?

GARY

Uh-huh...

WOMAN

Good night, Gary.

GARY

Good night... **Shelly.**

As they drift to sleep we

Fade to black

15

The Most Depressing Day in a Single Man's Life

It's 12:30 on a rainy Saturday night.

You've just been best man at your college flatmate's wedding.

Your ex-girlfriend sat at the next table.

With her fiancé.

Who's taller than you are, wealthier than you are, graduated from Oxford, swims, skis, sails, sculpts, recently appeared in *Arena*, has a full head of hair, co-founded a small transatlantic airline, and in his spare time raises funds for charity, hunts big game, and plays rhythm guitar for *Talking Heads*.

There also wasn't enough food to eat.

Half-drunk, blind with rage, you stagger home, buying the Sunday paper, a pound of designer ice cream (Gelato-Louis-Vuitton-Oreo-something at £15 a pound), and then tumble into your king-size bed.

Alone.

There were no messages on your machine.

There was no mail.

And you've lost the packet of matches where you scribbled down that sweet bridesmaid's telephone number.

Hoping to cheer yourself up with the latest news from 'The Mansion,' you reach for a copy of *Playboy*.

And there, on page 226, is Miss June.

She's pretty.

She's perfect.

She's pouting.

Vision of satin sheets, tumbling flesh, the gray-blue shadows of her eyes, and her mouth half open at dawn rush through your head.

You're happy.

And as you study the Playmate fact sheet, noting that she lists her interests as horseback riding, quiet romantic evenings in snow-bound cabins, making love in the surf, and listening to Jackson Browne, you suddenly come upon the single and most devastating piece of information ever to hit you before.

For the first time ever, a *Playboy* centrefold is younger than you are.

You could be dating these girls.

And the problem is that you're not dating these girls.

No matter what, *don't turn on the TV*.

Because you're only likely to see Gary Lineker, Ivan Lendl, or George Michael.

Who are also younger than you are.

And thus another set of dreams is shattered.

Yes, this is the point when you're finally forced to grow up.

The day when you stop reading *Playboy*.

And finally take out that subscription to *The Economist*.★

★As bad as this may seem, things *could* be worse. Consider the single most depressing day in any married man's life. That brilliant Saturday afternoon in October when the wind is crisp, his wife is beautiful, and he drives by the Porsche salesroom only to realize 'No. At this point, I really need something bigger and more practical.'

16

The Most Depressing Day in a Single Woman's Life

It's 4:00 on a Sunday afternoon.

You've just attended your best friend's baby's christening.

Which coincided with the publication of her first novel.

In the middle of the afternoon her husband announced he'd just been made senior political correspondent for *The Times*.

You dumped him in your first year at university.

And when you congratulated them on their good fortune, they thanked you for 'making it at all possible.'

There was plenty of food to eat.

But you downed six Bloody Marys instead.

Half-drunk, blind with rage, you drive home, passing what appear to be six thousand shiny brand-new couples entwined at every street corner and traffic light.

You lose a heel tripping up the front steps to your studio flat.

There are no messages on your machine.

There is no food in your fridge.

And you can't find the phone number of that divorced stock broker who called earlier in the week for a blind date.

Flopping onto your queen-size bed, you realize it's too late to go shopping, it's too early to go to bed, *Dynasty* isn't on for three hours yet, and the Meryl Streep film you wanted to see is no longer running.

Desperate for comic relief, you open the latest issue of *Cosmo* and begin to read this month's variation on the article about all the sensitive, caring, intelligent men there are in the world, and how the writer had oral sex with seventeen of them.

Which is when the phone rings.

No, it's not Mel Gibson.

It's not Harrison Ford.

It's not even the stockbroker.

It's your mother.

'How was the christening?'

'Fine, mum. I bought the kid a baby buggy.'

'It's funny,' your mother waxes. 'Do you realize that at your age I'd already had both you and your sister – and you were both at nursery school?'

Hanging up you debate about calling your therapist but realize things haven't been the same since he made a pass at you two weeks ago. So you call your girlfriends instead, and find out they all have dinner dates.

Arriving at your office twenty minutes later (passing another six thousand shiny new couples on the way and stopping to pick up some designer chocolate chip cookies – Famous Mrs David's 'fields of chocolate-chip something' at £45 a pound), you begin work on that 'really important' presentation that isn't due for another six months.

There is no heat.

There are no lights.

And just as you finally get the computer working you find the note from your boss saying your assistant – his nephew – has already finished the report.

Which is also just when you get your period, and your little sister rings to announce that she's getting engaged.

Yes, this particular Sunday is the day you learn that living well – or living at all – is the art of graceful compromise.

So you ring your mother back and tell her it's okay to give your number to Raymond, the wedding dress salesman your parents met on holiday last summer.

But she tells you he's already engaged.

Hanging up, you realize there is no justice in this world – only food, a job, cable television, and somebody else's boy-friend.

Not surprisingly, this is the day when you stop reading *Cosmo*. And you, too, finally take out that subscription to *The Economist*.*

---

*Again, just to look on the brighter side of things, consider the single most depressing day in any married man's life: That horrible Thursday night – just before midnight – when she realizes that her diaphragm can double as a contact lens holder – and that's *exactly* what it's been doing for the past six months. There's still no justice in this world – only food, a job, and somebody else's sex life.

17

Peaks and Valleys:
Time vs. Emotions

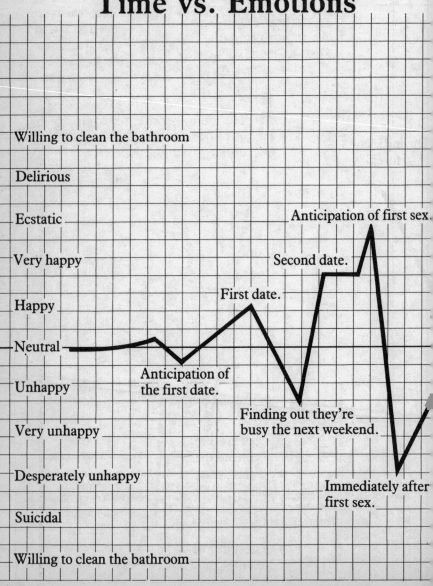

Willing to clean the bathroom

Delirious

Ecstatic

Anticipation of first sex.

Very happy

Second date.

Happy

First date.

Neutral

Anticipation of
the first date.

Unhappy

Finding out they're
busy the next weekend.

Very unhappy

Desperately unhappy

Immediately after
first sex.

Suicidal

Willing to clean the bathroom

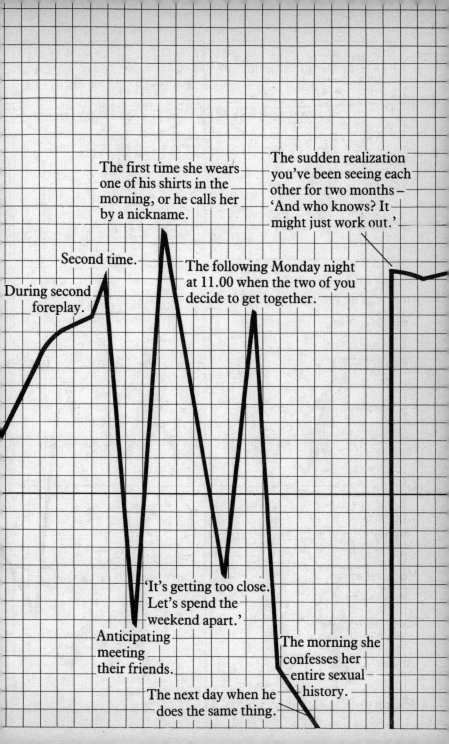

18

A Few Words About Freudian Analysis and Other Indoor Winter Sports

Overheard in a health club:

'I hate these people. They try to keep up with every trendy sport – tennis, jogging, aerobics, analysis . . .'

'Wait a minute. Analysis?'

'Sure. But the reason most of them gave it up is because they couldn't meet anybody doing it.'

As a general rule of thumb, never trust anybody who's been in therapy for more than 15 percent of their life span.

The words 'I am sorry' and 'I am wrong' will have totally disappeared from their vocabulary.

They will stab you, shoot you, break things in your home, say horrible things to your friends and family, and then justify this abhorrent behaviour by saying:

'Sure, I put your dog in the microwave. But *I feel better* for doing it.'

19

Meeting Their Friends

You say your new girlfriend's oldest girlfriend – Susan – has a voice that sounds like Godzilla on helium?

And that Larry – your new boyfriend's oldest mate – has all the charm of a mass murderer?

Yes, sooner or later, we all meet 'the in-laws' – the friends, university cronies, and old school pals who, in today's rootless society, have become the modern-day equivalent of the nuclear family.

(God, that sounds like something out of a sociology text book, doesn't it?)

Now admittedly, at first exposure, your new boyfriend's oldest friend – Kevin McCulloch – may seem toxic.

And you may be 100 percent accurate in observing that Chris – the old next-door neighbour and former member of the Rajneesh commune – barks at furniture and seems as shallow as a hot bath.

But don't say it. Under no circumstances should you mention these minor character flaws to your newly beloved.

Instead, bring these people into your life. Embrace them and cultivate them as friends. Invite them to dinner, take them along to see a film, and if they're single, try to fix them up with potential mates.

Why?

Three reasons:

First of all, they've been around longer than you have, and your new boyfriend or girlfriend will take your rejection of them as a personal affront. (Sorry to say it, but in the general scheme of things, the blood pact Alan and Peter performed twenty-five years ago at Scout Camp is still more important than the two blissful weeks you and Alan have recently spent in bed together.)

Second, because we live in basically insecure times, their assessment of you will be critical. You want them to like you – especially if you have any hopes of making the relationship work. (In my own case, I can remember once mentioning to a friend that 'Sheila was okay, but her IQ hovers somewhere around room temperature' – and bang – Sheila was history the next day.)

And finally, third, and most important, never forget that you need these people.

What for?

Think about the future.

How else are you going to find out what's going on after the two of you have broken up?

20

Drugs and Romance: Why Things Don't Go Better With Coke

There was a point in my life when I fell in love with a coke freak,'
Steven sighed, glancing out the tea-shop window.

'Half the time she was witty and glittery and charming and elusive
and bright, and insisted "I don't do drugs. . . ."*

'And the other half she turned into a pathological liar with mood
swings that would make Maummar al-Gaddafi proud – and was
borrowing money to buy them.'

Steven paused, sipping from his cup.

'How did it end, you ask?

'No matter what I did, I couldn't get her to stop. She was driving
me crazy, and I finally woke up one morning and realized –

'It costs me £210 a night to go out with Leslie . . .

'£70 for dinner.

'£70 for coke.

'And £70 for my therapist the next day.'

Steven stood, finished with lunch.

'And besides – how much fun do you think it is to peel somebody
off the ceiling every night at 3:00 in the morning?'

---

*For the record, it should be noted that the phase 'I don't do drugs' is perhaps the
most incredibly hip thing you can say in the eighties. The only way to surpass this –
and increase your coolness quotient – is to become a professional athlete or major
television star, and then annonce to the Press that you 'once had a major drug problem
but kicked it.'

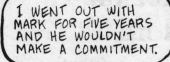

21

Advice for the Lovelorn

Somebody for Everybody?

Dear Sirs: I read several chapters back that there are four and a half billion people in the world. I've also read that there's somebody out there for everybody. Help! What if the woman who's perfect for me is working in a bean and curd factory in Shanghai? – An international telephonist, Coventry, England.

Dear International telephonist: In the end you have to believe in fate: minor car accidents, wrong phone numbers – the idea that eventually you're going to see the light at the end of the tunnel, and with luck it won't be a train. In researching your letter, we contacted a Miss Kim Dae Jung of the We're Marching Resolutely Into the Twenty-first Century, All Hail the Profit Motive, Who Was Mao? People's Bean Curd Collective (Ltd.) of Shanghai. She said she had absolutely no interest in meeting an international telephonist from Coventry, England. What can I say? On the other hand, sometimes it *is* a train.

Gift Etiquette

Sirs: I realize relationships don't last quite as long these days – but I'm a 'traditional kind o' bloke', and believe in celebrating anniversaries. What are the appropriate gifts?

Emlyn Jones, Cardiff, Wales.

Dear Emlyn: Modern romances require modern gifts. The first month is Velcro; the second is video tape; the third is microwave-safe cooking utensils. Beyond that, you're on your own. Just stick to impersonal items and nonstrategic metals and you should do fine.

Modern Manners

Sirs: When my boyfriend and I arrive at a restaurant, I expect him to get out of the car, walk around to my side, and open the door. I say it's good manners; he says I'm acting like Blanche Dubois. Am I crazy, or what? – Stuck in a Ford Zephyr, Taunton, Somerset.

Dear Stuck: You're crazy.

Youth Wants to Know

Sirs: About that last letter: Are these problems for real? Do people actually write in with these questions? It's something I've always wondered about advice columns. If they're real, why is the writing pattern and tone of voice always the same? How do you always manage to come up with such snappy answers? Is there some secret? Hoping you can solve this mystery, I remain – Still Stuck in a Ford Zephyr, Taunton Somerset.

Dear Stuck: It's no mystery at all. We make the letters up.

22

Desperately Seeking Someone: The Classified Ads

> **Dream-boat:** Beneath this elegant grey Rolls-Royce exterior beats the engine of a Ferrari. Not too many miles on this kid. Want to go out for a spin? Serious inquiries only. . . .
> – a singles ad in a national magazine

> **Dream-boat:** Rare, exotic beauty; a real head-turner. Great body. Loves long country rides, but happy on city streets. Nonsmoker. Is there room in your garage for me? Serious inquiries only. . . .
> – an ad for a '51 Ford

Is it really possible to find true love the same way you'd find a second-hand car?

Or, put another way:

Are you an 'affectionate, well-bred, fertile sexy female; a Company Director who's looking for love, romance, and good times? Do you like long walks on the beach and candle-lit dinners for two? Are you the kind of person who'd never take out or answer one of these ads? Are you funny, warm, vulnerable, and sensitive, sometimes crazy, always interesting?'

Or are you built more along the lines of a sexy male. City executive, jock/stud type, licensed pilot, Ryan O'Neal lookalike, mountain climber/Olympic skier/prize-winning journalist who hates bars and the singles scene? Do you like modern art, Laurie Anderson, and long romantic walks on the beach?

97

Jesus. Why don't we ever meet these people in real life?

Part of the explanation is that these ads are like abbreviated CVs – and just as 'leader of youth groups' on a CV translates to 'Scout leader,' and 'firsthand knowledge of penal institutions' usually means 'two to five years' grand larceny, suspended sentence,' the same kind of double-speak exists in the classifieds. Take these two:

> **Male Adonis** seeks sensual independent woman with traditional values, age 28–35. I'm a dedicated professional who likes Elvis Costello, Bach, museums, and long walks on the beach. Are you understanding, passionate and spontaneous? Let's be partners. All replies held in confidence.

And:

> **Cute, vivacious,** successful old-style girl with traditional values seeks sensual, self-assured man, age 32–40. Equally at home in pearls or jeans, looking for Mr Right who'll share London, Paris, jogging. Are you understanding, passionate, and spontaneous? Let's be partners. All replies held in confidence.

Okay. Here's how to read between the lines:

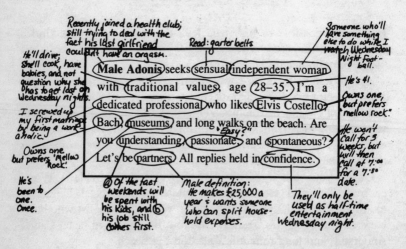

98

And:

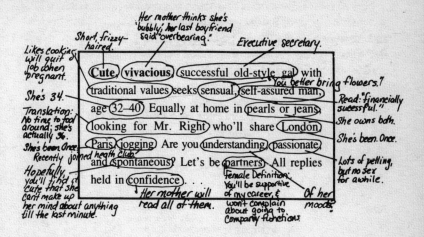

Obviously, the key phrases vary from ad to ad.

'Witty' usually means 'I can imitate Billy Crystal's "You look maahvelous," or "I own the Comic Relief album".'

A 'gentleman' is '45+, recently divorced, and terrified to make a move on the first date.' (Also read Volvo, boring.)

'Stunning beauty' means 'lots of makeup.'

'Sensitive' is 'five years of therapy.'

'Jazz lover' translates to 'I have a beard.' (Yes, women too.)

And 'Lives 20 minutes outside of the city' always means only one thing: 'geographically undesirable.'

But as telling as these euphemisms may be, perhaps the most interesting aspect of singles ads is how often you can read one, and understand *exactly* why somebody is still single. Here are two examples, reprinted just as they appeared in national magazines:

> **You are a female model** – 23–27. I am a safe, successful white businessman, 45, seeking a beautiful, gorgeous, blue-eyed intelligent blonde (5'6" or taller), for long walks on the beach and meaningful discussions about politics, theatre, the arts. Actresses okay too. I'll be supportive of your unique life-style.

And:

> **Stunning red-headed female Goddess,**
> thin, with incredible body, seeks
> financially secure Greek God for in-
> telligent relationship and long walks on
> the beach. Must be in good shape, over
> 6', and have a full head of hair. No
> smokers, no nutters. Photo a must. . . .

Come on. Are these people joking? Did they skip the year in school where we learn that looks aren't everything? If they're going to go this far, why not go the whole nine yards and advertise as follows:

> **Rich, sensitive, well-hung stud** seeks
> intelligent slut to take to the opera. Must
> be thin, beautiful, a good cook, excellent
> mother, and published in *The Economist*.
> Let's share romantic walks on the beach
> and romantic candle-lit dinners dis-
> cussing the new tax laws. Send your
> latest Helmut Newton photo-spread
> from *Vogue* and copy of your Nobel
> citation to . . .

And:

> **Oxford Double First**/whore in bed seeks
> Company chairman/David Soul lookalike/
> Cambridge Blue for a sensitive, down to
> earth relationship, complete with long
> walks on the beach, children (2), and
> live-in help. (At least 2.) No unreasonable
> expectations. Send copy of your first
> novel to . . .

In the end the question remains: Is it really possible to find true love the same way you'd find a second-hand car?

Have you ever noticed that every ad mentions something about wanting to take 'long romantic walks on the beach'?

All I know is one thing:

If just half of those ads had been successful, by now we would have paved the sand.

23

Obsessions

'If you love somebody, set them free'

– Sting

'. . . And if they don't come running back,
hunt them down and shoot them.'

– The Hell's Angels

Occasionally, we all 'go Latin.'

You know – you fall madly, instantly, totally in love with somebody, and all logic, balance, and self-respect go right out the window.

You find yourself saying things like 'I love the way you do the dishes!'

Or 'My God! We use the same shampoo!'

And next thing you know, the object of these affections has booked a seat on the next available Concorde –

Out of the country.

Out of the hemisphere.

Out of your life.

And next thing you know after that, you're lying there at night hugging the pillow, pretending it's Alan, Robin, Adam, or Lindsay; you're reading their horoscopes in *Cosmo*, praying it'll say 'FOOL! GO BACK! SANDY LOVES YOU!' and you start having those protracted fantasy conversations in the shower where Marion,

Bonnie, Clive, Johnny, Chuck or Amanda come rushing back, realizing that they never really gave you a chance.

If you find yourself caught up in this kind of obsession, book yourself on the next available Concorde –

To Mexico.

There's just no percentage in chasing after people who don't want us. It's hard on the ego, it ruins your chances of meeting somebody else, and sooner or later your friends will get tired of hearing about how badly the other person treated you.

Remember.

If somebody says 'I need space,' they mean it.

If somebody says 'You're suffocating me,' they mean it.

If somebody says 'I hate you and I never want to see you again,' they mean this too.

And if a relationship can be summed up with a film title like *Romancing the Stone, Sunday Bloody Sunday*, or *The Long Goodbye*, just give up – and don't sit there hoping these people will come back.

Because they never do.

Why not?

Because they don't.

(Sorry, but this is one of the few times in your adult life when you're going to have to take 'because' for an answer. There's no rational explanation for this behaviour; it's one of the mysteries of the universe that modern science has never been able to unravel, along with why spaghetti always tastes better cold the next morning, why we always get seated on the aeroplane next to the twenty stone woman who reeks of garlic, and why – after sex – when we go to the bathroom to get a glass of water, we always fill it to the top, drink half of it, refill it, and then return to the bedroom only to drink the rest.)

Now admittedly, this assessment – this total lack of hope – may seem bleak when you're in the middle of one of these relationships. But there is a bright side.

As Oscar Wilde said, 'When the gods wish to punish us, they answer our prayers.'

Consider the testimony of a woman who was obsessed with a man for five years, and then got him, only to complain:

'I feel like a dog who's been chasing a car.

'I chased and chased and chased . . .

'And the only problem is that when I finally caught him, I was still a dog, and he was still a car. . . .

'And now I haven't got the slightest idea what to do with him.'

24

Little Known
Facts of Romance

- Among certain nations along the Ivory Coast 'standing someone up' is considered a crime punishable by death.
- The average date lasts 3.697 hours, consumes 10 fluid ounces of alcoholic beverages, costs £25, and usually destroys at least one 'really good' item of clothing.
- It's illegal to double-date in Liechtenstein during July.
- Approximately 19.7 million women lost their virginity to the song 'Stairway to Heaven' during the mid-seventies.
- In certain parts of the country, playing music by Rick James after midnight is considered lewd and lascivious behaviour.
- There is no word in Swahili for panty hose.
- The International Bureau of Statistics has estimated that enough mouthwash is consumed each year in the process of preparing for a date to fill the area of Lake Windermere.
- Benito Mussolini was not a good dancer.
- And despite spending billions each year in exercise facilities, supposedly building up their pectorals and laterals, millions of politically apathetic singles have not yet realized one simple fact:
- Jane Fonda did not meet Tom Hayden in a health club.

25

The Greatest Lies of Extra-marital Affairs

'Sure, I know he's married. But believe me, I can handle it.'

'I'm going to leave her next weekend.'

'That's okay. I don't mind spending Christmas alone.'

'I'm going to leave her next month.'

'That's okay. I don't mind spending New Year's Eve alone.'

'I can't leave her right now, the kid is sick.'

'That's okay. I don't mind spending the August Bank Holiday alone.'

'I can't leave her right now. She's too weak.'

'I'm going to kill myself.'

'We'll spend next weekend together.'

'I promise you, it's not just sex. I'm leaving her.'

'I need to know when.'

'Right after the holidays.'

'I don't mind spending Christmas alone.'

'I don't mind spending New Year's alone.'

'I know what I said, but I owe it to her I just can't throw eleven years of marriage out the window.'

'I'm never going to put myself through anything like this again.'

'I'm terribly sorry, Miss . . . I'm such a clumsy idiot . . . I didn't mean to spill the drink on you.'

'Sure, I know he's married. But believe me, this time I can handle it.'

26

Meeting Their Parents

Essentially, all serious relationships progress in the same fundamental manner:

1) You go out.
2) You go to bed.
3) You go to meet their parents.

Yes, sooner or later we all get dragged to a wedding, Christmas party, or even a funeral.

Contrary to popular myth, these events were not created to bring families together in some kind of warm-spirited communal setting.

In truth, they were designed, conceived, and strategically spaced throughout the year solely to give parents the chance to look over their children's prospective mates.

(Yes, even funerals. Although in this case, if the deceased happens to be your girlfriend's mother, her vote on you is already cast.)

Now obviously it would be easier (and less stressful) to meet someone's parents on more neutral turf like centre pitch at a football match or some other event that cuts down on small talk – a natural disaster of epic proportions or Johannesburg High School's annual Martin Luther King Day celebration.

But just because you lack the home-court advantage doesn't mean these affairs can't be put to your own good use.

1) *Check out the relatives.*

Look around the dinner table:

Is there an obvious history of early senility in the family?

Bad manners?

Terrible feuds?

Feckless in-laws who'll ask for money?

'Every unhappy family is unhappy in its own way,' wrote Tolstoy in *Anna Karenina*.

This may be true, but once the novelty wears off, who wants to be part of it?

2) *Get a close look at mum and dad.*

How are they holding up?

How's the skin tone?

The muscle structure?

Theoretically, this is what you're going to be waking up next to in thirty-five years.

Remember: A health club may do wonders for a twenty-eight-year-old, but the basic DNA's are for keeps.

3) *Scrutinize the parent/child relationship.*

Is she still 'daddy's little girl'?

Is he sycophantically attached to mum?

This can only lead to major trouble along the road.

Not only will you have permanent lunch guests, but worse, you'll find yourself forever trying to live up to mummy and daddy – which can be exceedingly difficult if daddy happens to be chairman of the board of Esso and mummy is on Valium.

Of course all this comes into play only if you're unsure about a given romance. If you truly care for someone, the object of the meeting is to make the parents like you. As such, an entirely different mode of behaviour is called for.

1) *Don't make a pass at either parent.*

A man should never try to sleep with his girlfriend's mother. (No matter how appreciative of this attention the mother may be, you want her to like you, but not quite in this fashion.)

A woman should never sit in her boyfriend's father's lap. (Neither heart attacks nor the sight of his wife brandishing a shotgun at the dinner table are good for the digestive system.)

And finally, a man should never sit in either his own father's or his date's father's lap. (The only exception to this rule is if the old man happens to be English aristocracy. These gentleman have always been known to harbour certain – well, latent tendencies. And said behaviour will not only enhance the size of your wedding present, but will also provide you with a stylish social life after the divorce.)

2) *Don't get rip-roaringly drunk like Aunt Rosie.*

The perils of consuming your host's entire supply of alcohol are self-explanatory. But it leads to an interesting anecdote:

Several years ago I was invited to have Christmas dinner with a new girlfriend's parents at their home. (In the woman's words, we were 'smitten' with each other.) Upon arriving, her father began to pour champagne like a Coca-Cola distributor who couldn't get rid of the new formula fast enough. Amid all the joviality, I accidentally dropped a £150 crystal champagne flute into a £25,000 Steinway grand piano. Her parents were not amused. And they were even less amused when I suggested they 'send the piano to a dry cleaners and send me the bill.' How was dinner, you ask? Wonderful. The airline served turkey on the flight back to London.

3) *Bring a present for the house.*

If you really want a relationship to work, part of the trick is to make his or her parents accept you as 'one of their own.' Nothing will accomplish this as fast as bringing flowers, wine, or chocolates the first time you're invited. Ingratiating yourself this way also offers one additional advantage: once they think of you as 'part of the family,' you can appear the second time with the same kind of presents their own children bring – your laundry or the children from your first marriage.

4) *And if you're staying the weekend:*

Don't even think about sleeping together. We may live in the twentieth-century but the minute you pass through the portals of a parent's house, you might as well have stepped back into seventeenth-century Tokugawa, Japan. You may be thirty-nine, twice divorced, and have been living together for six years, but in most cases there's just no way someone's parents are going to sanction you doing it – in sin – under their roof.

Why?

First, they find the idea of the two of you naked in bed together just about as incomprehensible as we find the idea of the two of them naked in bed together.

And second, think about your own parents.

Remember all those years ago when you had that little heart-to-heart talk about where you lost your virginity?

Twenty years later, no one's parents have ever got over the fact that one of their kids lost it in their bed.

27

Why You Should Never Go Out With a Yuppie

My friend David could barely contain his excitement.

'Quick!' he roared over his car phone (installed in 1985), 'you've got to meet me at my house! I've just bought the ultimate status symbol of the eighties!'

Forever on the lookout for important cultural milestones, I immediately drove over to David's house, assuming that I'd find him preening over some expensive new toy. But when I arrived in the drive not fifteen minutes later, the scene was exactly the opposite of what I'd expected. He was sobbing inconsolably, beating his fists on the roof of his black turbo-charged Porsche.

'What's wrong?' I cried out, rushing to his side.

'Look!' David wailed, and pointed to the roof of his post-modernist penthouse conversion (1982). And there, just above his thermal heating panels (1982), I saw it for the first time: a massive white dish, upturned towards the sky.

For half a second I wondered if we'd been invaded by alien kitchenware from another planet, but knew this couldn't be the case.

'Okay,' I said finally. 'I give up. What is it? A solar-powered wok?'

David glared at me through his tears. 'Don't you know *anything*?' he snarled. 'Chinese food is out. *That*,' he explained, 'happens to be a satellite TV dish. It's the latest thing. It costs £7,000 and brings in 27,000 channels. You can watch sports, *Hogan's Heroes*, and *The Love Boat* twenty-four hours a day. You can see Mickey Rourke and Kim Basinger in *9½ Weeks* virtually around the clock.'

I considered this for a moment. 'I can understand what you'd be upset about,' I said at last. 'I mean, having that thing on your roof, and paying £7,000 to watch *9½ Weeks*.

'No, no, no,' David interrupted. 'It's not my dish that bothers me.' He pointed across the street. 'It's *theirs*!'

Sure enough, there was another solar-powered wok sitting atop another post-modernist penthouse conversion across the street. But before I could express my condolences, David had begun to pound the Porsche again. (Which, incidentally, was purchased in 1985, replacing a Saab, replacing a BMW, replacing a Volvo, replacing a VW Beetle with a CND sticker in the rear window.)

'Let's go in the house and discuss this,' I said, putting my arm around his shoulders.

'That's a good idea,' David sniffled. 'Besides, we should get out of the sun. It gives you cancer.'

Inside, we stepped into the cool darkness of his black media room (1982), where David began to pace back and forth between his large-screen TV (1977), his Betamax (1978), his compact disc player (1984), and his home computer (1982, used exactly once).

'I just can't keep up anymore,' he groaned. 'Every time I think I'm ahead – every time I think I'm on the cutting edge – they catch up.'

To prove his point, he threw open his two-inch silver, matt blinds (1982).

'Look! There are hundreds of dishes! All over the neighbourhood!'

Sure enough, he was right again – almost every post-modernist penthouse in the development now had a £7,000 electronic rain catcher plopped on the roof. Glancing over the vista, however, I also noticed that something else had changed: David's lush basil garden was gone. Being a longtime fan of pesto, I asked why.

'Pesto's over,' he announced. 'I ripped out the garden and put in garlic bulbs.'

Standing there, it suddenly occurred to me that David had the personality of a human Rubik's Cube: he was forever twisting and turning, forever unable to come up with the right pattern.

'You've got to get your mind off this stuff,' I told him, and quickly suggested we use his tennis court (1975), his sauna (1976), the Jacuzzi (1977), his home gym (bicycle, 1980, rowing machine, 1981, Nautilus machine, 1984), or even his lap pool (1985).

But he just as quickly dismissed each as either being 'passé' or 'last year's idea.'

'Well, how about a drink,' I said at last. 'A simple drink?'

David agreed, and the two of us walked into his black Phoggenphol kitchen, complete with Pirelli floors (1981), and an antique French country table (1982; a brief aberration). He paused in front of his glass-doored Sub-Zero commercial refrigerator (1984) and asked what I'd like to drink.

'Got a Coke?'

He handed me an orange-flavoured Perrier.

'I just don't know what I'm going to do,' he said, leaning against his collection of herbal vinegars (1981–1984). 'The way I see it, it's just impossible to maintain your individuality in today's society.'

Glancing around the room at his microwave (1976), convection oven (1977), Cuisinart (1978), pasta machine (1979), gelato maker (1980), espresso steamer (1983), Braun coffee grinder (1984), and Thai cookbook (1985), I decided more drastic action was required. I chose my words carefully.

'David,' I said quietly, 'have you ever considered that you need more people in your life instead of more gadgets? Like a wife? Or friends? Or a family?'

He pondered this concept. Briefly. I watched his face turn from sorrow to contemplation to outright joy and exultation in less than fifteen seconds. The idea seemed to root, grow, and blossom in roughly the same time it took the dressmakers to put out their replica of the royal wedding dress.

'That's it!' he exclaimed. 'You're absolutely right! I need friends! I need people!' Beaming, he reached into a drawer. 'And I've got just the phone to call them with!'

Quick as you could say 'Let's jam the exchange,' the contraption was on the table.

'Look,' he said. 'It dials 37,000 numbers automatically and records up to twelve years of incoming messages!'

Things were not proceeding quite as I expected.

'Did anybody call?'

David rewound the machine, then fell silent.

'No.'

'Exactly my point. You keep buying all this stuff to make you happy – all these gadgets – but the truth is that you're just lonely, and it hurts.'

David's eyes lit up like cats eyes in the middle of the road.

'You're right!' he cried, reminding me of the way he'd suddenly discovered it at est (1974). 'I'm lonely! I hurt!' He paused, narrowing his eyes. 'And I know just the thing I can buy to solve it!'

Before I could stop him, David was frantically searching his kitchen drawers for a phone number. Gadgets flew everywhere: Walkmans, Swatches, hand-held video games, pocket calculators . . .

But by now I'd given up.

Alas, even a human Rubik's Cube gets tiring.

But as I walked out the door I couldn't help but overhear his phone call:

'Hello, Doc? . . . It's David. Remember me? . . . Great. Now about that artificial heart . . .'

Sex!

The Complete History of Sex:

Sex was invented by Thomas Alva Edison on July 16, 1876.

At the time, Edison had been working to develop 'entertainment devices' for the masses – and during the previous months he had invented the whoopee-cushion, the hand-buzzer, Play-Doh, fake-nose spectacles, the first cordless vibrator (a massive steam-powered unit that covered six and a half square city blocks and required 235 men to operate), and the one device he considered to be his greatest gift to mankind at the time: the ball-point pen that turned over to reveal a naked woman.

Upon being introduced to sex, the country was thrown into turmoil – and in order to maintain order, the government seized all of Tom's patents and drawings, and locked them away in the historical archives until the year 2186. (The only exception to this were his plans for the steam-powered vibrator, which were released in 1964 and used as the basic design for the nuclear submarine USS *Trident*.)

Devastated at the havoc he'd created, Edison redoubled his efforts to provide entertainment for the masses and quickly invented films, the mimeograph, and the phonograph.

In fact, his greatest invention of all, the light bulb, was created as a means of deterring sex.

Because as Tom himself put it, 'Who in God's name would ever want to do it with the lights on?'

28

The Three Greatest Lies of Sex

1) 'Size doesn't count.'

2) Spermicidal jelly has no taste.'

3) 'No. Really. I don't mind. Honestly.
   It just felt good to have you inside me.'

29

On Sleeping
with Strangers

Sooner or later, it happens to all of us.

You meet somebody, you're attracted, the hormones get to work, and next thing you know it's two-thirty in the morning, you've checked into the Hilton, and you're flailing around a king-size bed performing acrobatic feats that would do the Flying Wallendas proud.

Do not hesitate. Do not feel guilty.

The fact is we all go astray once in a while.

So calm down, take a deep breath, and do not panic.

Your body is better than you imagine.

The other person is just as vulnerable, just as insecure, and just as worried about making strange noises as you are.

And the odds are you've used *some* discretion – you're not leaping into bed with Jerry Cottle's entire animal act, Charles Manson, a guy who yells 'Down, Simba!' or some woman who's nickname is Disease du Jour.

So lay back (or turn over) and enjoy yourself.

At best, you may learn a new technique or wake up with somebody you'll actually come to know and like over time.

And at worst, you can take heart in one simple fact:

It's entirely possible to spend *five years* in a relationship with someone and still wake up one morning only to find yourself in bed with a total stranger.

30

Speaking in Tongues, or What Ever Happened to Kissing?

The clink of ice cubes. The thwack of a diving board. A Sunday newspaper ruffles in the August breeze.

'It's strange,' Michael says, shifting his deckchair under the white sun. 'I love Jamie, but it doesn't seem to be getting anywhere. Even in bed. She loves sex, but she doesn't seem to like kissing me.'

Tom folds down the business section. He glances across the sun-drenched lawn. He watches Jamie pull herself out of the pool: tan hands on the chrome ladder, rivulets of water rushing down her limbs, tracing the arteries in her arms and legs.

'The explanation is simple,' Tom says, turning to Friday's closing prices in the City. 'Sex is a biological function. Kissing is a commitment.'

More Great Lies of Sex

1) 'I've never done this before.'

2) 'I've done this only once before.'

3) 'I don't usually act like this.'

4) 'I never come the first time I'm in bed with anybody.'

5) 'I could never have sex with two different people on the same day.'

6) 'Come on. Nobody's going to see these pictures but us.'

7) 'This has only happened to me once before.'

8) 'I bought the Porsche because of the way it drives.'

9) 'I love you too.'

Yet Another Trip
to the Pictures:
Strange Bedfellows

The scene is a single man's bedroom with a perfect, stellar view of the South Bank, with a million sparkling lights in the distance. It's 1:30 in the morning, dead winter. Snowing. The door opens and KAREN enters, barefoot and in a black evening dress. SIMON is directly behind her, dress shirt open at the neck. Both carry champagne glasses and feel the happy-tired electricity of a romance about to begin. There's a giddiness in the air as they walk to the windows. . . . The night is old, but still young.

KAREN: I can't believe you found a place like this. The view is incredible.

SIMON: Yeah . . . sometimes I sit up here late at night and look out at the lights and think, 'Someday . . . none of this will be yours.'

KAREN (*chuckling*): How'd you find it, anyway?

SIMON: It was easy – I just had to promise the estate agent my firstborn child.

KAREN: A boy or a girl?

SIMON: A girl. He's going to pick her up when she's seventeen. (*Sips his champagne.*) Actually, the view has one drawback – it's so bright that it's impossible to fall asleep . . . so every night I have to ring every one of the people in every one of those buildings and ask them to turn off their lights. . . . My phone bill is extraordinary.

KAREN: I had no idea you lived under such hardship.

She appreciates the joke and sips from her champagne glass. They take in the view together, small against the diamond-lights and concrete.

KAREN: When I was a little girl I always dreamed about moving to the city, having a view like this. It's so grown-up. . . . It's really beautiful.

SIMON (*turns to her, closely*): No. . . . You are.

He kisses her. Softly at first, like a snowflake at Christmas. They then embrace fully.

KAREN: Something tells me you've done this before.

SIMON: I bet you say that to all the guys. . . . (*Kissing again.*) I just don't want you to think you're going to take advantage of me. . . (*Another kiss.*) I'm not that kind of guy. I'm saving myself for my second wife.

KAREN: You were married?

SIMON: I don't think so . . . but there's a period at university that's really blurred.

She laughs, and he kisses her again.

KAREN: Simon . . . we shouldn't. . . .

SIMON (*running his finger along her cheek*): Karen, Karen . . . They say there are three kinds of 'no's' in this world – the no that means 'no' the no that means 'yes' and the no that means 'convince me.'

KAREN (*wryly*): Which one did I just give you?

SIMON: I think you need some more convincing.

He kisses her. She responds, and they move to the bed, hand in hand, mouth on mouth. As they lie on the pillow, giggling, nipping at each other, a sixty-year-old woman materializes out of the shadows. It's KAREN'S MOTHER. Tough. Chain-smoking. She perches on the bedside table.

KAREN'S MOTHER: Christ. I can't believe I brought you up to behave like this. Haven't you learned your lesson with men like this yet?

Karen looks up. Simon is unaware of her mother's presence.

SIMON: Is something wrong?

KAREN: No. . . . Never mind.

KAREN'S MOTHER (*as they resume kissing*): It's lucky your father's not alive to see this. It would kill him.

SIMON: You taste so nice. . . .

KAREN'S MOTHER: I think I'm going to be sick.

As Simon kisses Karen's neck, a second, younger woman materializes on the other side of the bed. She's SIMON'S OLD GIRLFRIEND. Both women watch the action.

SIMON: It's strange. . . . The first time I ever saw you, all I wanted to do was hold you and kiss you. . . . I don't remember the last time I felt like that.

SIMON'S OLD GIRLFRIEND: That's funny – I remember it exactly: June 16, 1983. In the house on Station Lane. Remember now?

Simon looks up momentarily, but goes back to kissing Karen.

SIMON: It's not like I say that to everybody.

SIMON'S OLD GIRLFRIEND: No. You choose your victims very carefully. If I recall correctly, your next line is:

(*She says this next line in unison with him.*)

SIMON: I wondered what it would be like to wake up with you in the morning.

SIMON'S OLD GIRLFRIEND: Waking up together one morning was easy. The rude awakening came six months later when you said getting up with me was like co-starring in *Dawn of the Dead*.

KAREN: That's so sweet. . . .

KAREN'S MOTHER: Sweet? If this gets any sweeter I'm going to suffer insulin shock. Karen – listen to me. You don't really believe this nonsense, do you?

KAREN (*To Simon, as he kisses her*): That feels great.

As Karen and Simon writhe on the sheets – with Simon kissing her neck –
a third presence appears: SIMON'S BEST FRIEND.

SIMON'S BEST FRIEND: Go for it, Simon! It's been too long! I'm all for it!

SIMON (*pausing thoughtfully*): You know, I really do like you. You're special.

SIMON'S BEST FRIEND: No! Don't say that! It's stupid! You want to get yourself into trouble?

As they continue, another presence appears at the foot of the bed:

KAREN'S FOUR BEST FRIENDS, *in wedding gowns, singing à la Beverley Sisters.*

KAREN'S FRIENDS (*they clap*): Because we're (*clap!*) goin' to the chapel, and we're (*clap!*) gonna get married. . . . Goin' to the chapel of love . . .

KAREN (*to Simon*): Mmmm. Don't stop.

As they continue kissing, yet another presence appears at the foot of the bed:

KAREN'S LAST BOYFRIEND: 'Don't stop'?!? What do you mean, 'Don't stop'?!? Stop was the only word you ever knew with me. Stop! Stop! We didn't go to bed for three months! You've been out with this guy – what – four times?

KAREN'S MOTHER: I told her she should have married you. But *no*. A nice gynaecologist from Bristol wasn't good enough for my daughter, Miss Career Woman.

SIMON'S OLD GIRLFRIEND: If I were you I'd get your daughter out of this bed. He's like the neutron bomb of relationships – the shell survives, but your insides are vaporized.

SIMON'S BEST FRIEND: Hey – I wouldn't talk. You were no dream come true either.

SIMON'S OLD GIRLFRIEND: Yeah? Well, maybe if he got over some of his infantile male-bonding fantasies – your football games and fishing trips.

SIMON'S BEST FRIEND: We could have taken you out shark fishing – but you don't eat your own kind.

KAREN'S LAST BOYFRIEND (*to Simon's old girlfriend*): I'm sorry to interrupt, but don't I know you from somewhere?
KAREN'S MOTHER: This is insane.

On the bed, they both seem distracted – but nevertheless proceed. Slightly out of breath, Simon reaches around to the back of Karen's dress.

SIMON: I think this is stuck.
KAREN: Let me help you.

As she reaches around, her best friends begin to sing:

KAREN'S FRIENDS: 'Tonight you're mine, completely. . . . You give your love so sweetly. . . . But will you love me tomorrow?'

As they kiss, two more people materialize: SIMON'S PARENTS.

SIMON'S FATHER: Go for it, Simon. Just like a chip off the old block. I'm proud of you, son.
SIMON'S BEST FRIEND: Me too.
SIMON'S MOTHER: Henry, how can you say that?
SIMON'S FATHER: Say what? It's good for him. He's a young guy. Maybe our marriage would have worked out better if *we'd* had more experience.
SIMON'S MOTHER: Don't get me started about experience. Being married didn't prevent you and that receptionist . . .
SIMON'S FATHER: Like I said. Our marriage might have worked out better.
SIMON'S MOTHER: But . . .
SIMON'S FATHER: I don't want to discuss it, Esther.
SIMON'S MOTHER: Fine. But that isn't the point. . . . That's our son in bed, taking advantage of some poor, innocent girl. . . . And this room . . . Simon – aren't you embarrassed? Don't you ever clean up?

Karen's in her slip; Simon starts to unbutton his shirt. Both are trying to concentrate, occasionally looking off at their detractors.

KAREN: Let me help you.

SIMON'S BEST FRIEND: I don't think she's so innocent.

SIMON'S OLD GIRLFRIEND: Neither is he.

KAREN'S LAST BOYFRIEND: Sluts of a feather . . .

SIMON'S MOTHER (*to the old boyfriend*): How *dare* you talk about my daughter like that. You're the one who walked out and broke her heart in the first place.

KAREN'S LAST BOYFRIEND: Jesus!

SIMON'S BEST FRIEND (*aside, to Karen's last boyfriend*): In the end, it's always us against them. If you want, I'll give you some of Simon's old numbers when this is over.

KAREN'S LAST BOYFRIEND: Who are you? Joel Grey?

SIMON'S OLD GIRLFRIEND: Take him up on it. They're *wonderful* girls. Just wear a surgical mask when you talk on the phone.

SIMON'S BEST FRIEND: I love you, too, kitten. Can I get you a saucer of milk?

SIMON'S OLD GIRLFRIEND: Nice comeback, Joel.

On the bed, Simon is on top of Karen. They're trying hard to concentrate, but can't; they're both looking off in different directions.

SIMON'S MOTHER: Simon, how can you do this? Do you always have to end up in bed with these girls?

SIMON'S FATHER: Esther, let's go home.

KAREN'S MOTHER: Come on, Karen. Get out of bed. Dump this idiot. He could be real bad news.

SIMON'S MOTHER: Bad News? What about your little tramp?

KAREN'S MOTHER: Don't start with me, you old bag. Why don't you take your husband home before he finds another receptionist?

SIMON'S MOTHER: Bitch!

KAREN'S MOTHER: Slut!

SIMON'S MOTHER: Whore!

SIMON'S BEST FRIEND: So far I give this round to Frazier, but Ali might take it on points.

SIMON: Karen?

KAREN'S MOTHER: Scum!

SIMON'S MOTHER: You're both disgusting.

KAREN'S LAST BOYFRIEND: I'll second that.

KAREN: Simon?

KAREN'S LAST BOYFRIEND (*to Simon's old girlfriend*): Do you want to get out of here and get something to drink?

KAREN'S GIRLFRIENDS (*Aretha Franklin! With dancing! And full orchestration!*): I said Think! (*chorus: Think, think!*) What you tryin' to do to me! I said Think! (*Think, think!*) And your mind can set you free! I said freedom. . . . (*Freedom!*) Freedom (*Freedom!*) Free –

SIMON (*Just as she's about to hit the high note*): Stop!

The room falls silent. Everyone stares as Simon sits up in bed and faces Karen.

SIMON: Look . . . I know we're both nervous, but . . .

KAREN: It's always hard the first time.

SIMON: I know . . . but the truth is that I do like you – and I really do want to be with you.

KAREN: Me too.

SIMON: Okay. In that case, close your eyes, take a deep breath, and calm down. Let's focus on being here.

They both close their eyes and breathe deeply. When they reopen their eyes a second later, the room is empty again.

SIMON: Feel better?

KAREN: Yes. What about you?

SIMON: Absolutely. (*Leaning against the headboard.*) Come 'ere.

She lies cradled in his arms, silent.

KAREN: Simon.

SIMON: What, Karen?

KAREN: Do you remember in First Year Psychology where they told you that every time you get into bed with somebody, you're geting into bed with all their old lovers, and their parents, and friends?

SIMON: Sure.

KAREN: Do you believe it?

SIMON (*a long hesitation*): No. Not a chance. (*Pauses.*) What about you?

KAREN: No. Me neither.

A sly grin passes between them.

SIMON: Do you want to start again?

KAREN: Remind me – what were the three 'no's'?

Simon smiles, reaches over. . . .

Kisses her. . . .

And turns out the light.

33

The Sheet Rule

Never trust anyone with more than three sets of bed sheets.
Why?

No matter how much they may claim to love cottons, florals, patterns, stripes, or solids, it all comes down to one thing.

Anyone with more than three sets of sheets is changing them too damn often.

Breaking Up

'They say that breakin' up is hard to do.'
— *Neil Sedaka*

'They're wrong.'

— *Clint Eastwood*

The Twelve Warning Signs That a Relationship Is on the Rocks

1) You get a lump in your throat or a hacking cough when you're supposed to say the words 'I love you.'
2) Small cuts and wounds cease to heal quickly.
3) A general lethargy sets in, and you find yourself 'too tired' to make that 11:30 Wednesday night 'let's sleep together' cross-town run.
4) At parties it feels as though you've got a 10-stone growth on your arm.
5) You get a clock-radio for your birthday.
6) Migraine headaches seem to develop whenever she uses the baby talk you formerly found attractive.
7) Dizziness and nausea set in at the sight of what you used to describe as his endearing habit of leaving his clothing on the floor.
8) A sense of anxiety settles in as you come across some of those old numbers in your address book.
9) You get depressed during sex because the only way you can make your partner come is by telling fantasy stories.
10) You wake up in the middle of the night in a cold sweat and realize there's enough room between the two of you to put in a three-lane motorway, two shopping centres, a Burger King and a NATO airforce base.

11) And yet you still feel claustrophobic.
12) For some unexplained reason, you wake up early on Sunday mornings with an unexplained desire to wash the car.

35

Grounds for Justifiable Homicide in Any Relationship

Remember the marshmallow defence?

The legal argument that a man couldn't be held responsible for a murder because he'd eaten so much junk food that his blood sugar had risen to the point where he was completely out of control?

In relationships there are a thousand ways somebody can commit grievous bodily harm on your psyche.

If anyone tries any one of the following manoeuvres with you, don't think twice about shooting them.

There isn't a jury in the land that'll convict you of murder.

Sometimes, after all, crimes of passion are merely acts of self-preservation.

You have just cause to shoot:

— Anyone who checks up on you by ringing and then hangs up at the first sound of your voice.

— Anyone who utters the words 'I love you but I'm not *in love* with you.'

— Anyone who won't be committed to a relationship but on the other hand won't leave you alone.

- Anyone you're in love with who insists on talking about all the other people they're seeing.

- Anyone who sighs 'I know that if I gave you half a chance I'd marry you.'

You have just cause to maim:

- Any woman you're in love with who opens a conversation by saying 'I rode my first Harley-Davidson this weekend.'

- Any man who answers the phone while you're in bed together.

- And finally, anyone – man, woman, boyfriend, or girlfriend – who invites you over to his or her house and then answers the phone more than twice with a hushed voice, saying, 'I can't talk now. I'll have to call you back later.'

The Greatest Lies
of Breaking Up

1) 'We have to talk.' (This actually means 'You have to listen', mostly to something you don't want to hear.)
2) 'This is just as difficult for me as it is for you.'
3) 'I wouldn't be saying this if I didn't really care about you.'
4) 'You didn't tell me.'
5) 'I didn't know.'
6) 'You're too good for me.'
7) 'I can't give you what you need.'
8) 'It's not you. It's me.'
9) 'I just can't fall in love with anybody right now.'
10) 'You'll see. It's better this way.'
11) 'You'll make someone a terrific wife.'
12) 'You deserve somebody better.'
13) 'You'll get over me.'
14) 'I'll never forget you.'
15) 'Come on. It's not the end of the world.'
16) 'Who knows? Maybe things'll be different in a couple of months.'
17) 'I promise I'll call next week to find out how you are.'

Revenge

'Don't get mad, get even.'

– Joseph P. Kennedy

'Don't get even, get jewelry.'

– Anon.

I feel like I've been in a hit-and-run car accident. I got hit, and she ran.'

'That's nothing. Martin pulled off so many stunts in the last year that Clint Eastwood invited him to join a professional stuntman's association.'

Upset?

Paralysed?

Have the feeling that you've just been pushed from the top of Centre Point?

They say that living well is the best revenge.

They're wrong.

Revenge is the best revenge.

And while we can all admire the woman who got even with an old flame by having *Hustler* and seventeen other homosexual publications sent to his office in the City.

Or the bloke who broke into his old girlfriend's flat while she was away on holiday, dialled 'Tim' in Tokyo, and left the phone off the hook for a month, running up a phone bill of £21,000.

The problem with these schemes is that they hurt only the bastard's pride (or wallet) and didn't get to the heart of the matter – meaning that they didn't inflict major damage to the soul.

If you really want to get even with someone, you're basically offered two alternative paths. First is the low road – the cruise-missile style – where you either a) sleep with their best friend or b) become incredibly rich, famous, and successful and then marry their best friend. (Obviously there are certain inherent risks here – like spending thirty years with somebody who's even worse than the person you were getting even with in the first place. Yet every cloud has its yellow-rain lining: You can become still richer, still more successful, and still more famous – and then divorce the best friend and continue to turn the knife by dating Victoria Principal or Don Johnson. Admittedly, it's a long way to go, but I'm sure Victoria and Don will be understanding.)

Then there's the mature path:

Do nothing.

Sit back, bide your time, and wait.

In the end, life has a way of getting even with all of us.

And just as the old adage 'Time heals all wounds' is true (yes, eventually you will recover), you can also take comfort in the fact that the other old adage is equally real:

Sooner or later, time wounds all heels.

38

Government Health Warning: Late-Night Radio Shows May Be Hazardous to Your Health

---

No matter where you live, the catharsis for breaking up with someone is always the same: you get-out on the motorway and drive.

For some unexplained reason, millions of otherwise sane people console themselves over lost love affairs by squandering insane amounts of precious fossil fuels on the open road.

Perhaps it has something to do with a sense of control: the idea that if we can't steer a relationship with a hundred odd pounds of flesh and blood in a particular direction, there's something oddly reassuring about turning a key, squeezing the accelerator to the floor, and having 4,000 pounds of steel, glass, and chrome respond instantly, going in whatever direction we want.

Petrol pump psychology aside, if you find yourself in this state of mind, there's one important thing to remember:

Do not listen to a late-night radio show.

Every song they play is number one with a bullet.

The problem is that they're all so depressing that after a half hour of listening, the bullet will be through your head.

For those of you who revel in gloom, here is a complete playlist of 'whispering' Bob Harris, John Peel and Tony Blackburn in his bitterer moments.

If nothing else, this lends new definition to the phrase 'counting down' the charts.

The Ultimately Depressing Top Forty

(as compiled by Smash Hits
and the Radio Request Show
at the Middlesex Hospital)

1.	The Way We Were	Barbra Streisand
2.	She's Out of My Life	Michael Jackson
3.	Weekend in New England	Barry Manilow
4.	Rainy Days and Mondays	The Carpenters
5.	It Don't Matter to Me	Bread
6.	Bridge Over Troubled Water	Simon and Garfunkel
7.	For No One	The Beatles
8.	If You Could Read My Mind	Gordon Lightfoot
9.	MacArthur Park	Richard Harris
10.	Killing Me Softly	Roberta Flack
11.	Walk Away Renee	The Left Bank
12.	I Keep Forgettin' (We're not in love anymore)	
		Michael McDonald
13.	Diamonds and Rust	Joan Baez
14.	Sometimes When We Touch	Dan Fogelberg
15.	Can't Live (If living is without you)	Harry Nillsson
16.	I'm Almost Over You	Sheena Easton
17.	If Ever You're in My Arms Again	Peabo Bryson
18.	She's Gone	Hall and Oates
19.	You've Lost That Lovin' Feeling	Righteous Brothers
20.	Always Something Breakin' Us in Two	Joe Jackson
21.	Where Were You When I Needed you Last Winter?	
		Stevie Wonder
22.	We've Got Tonight	Kenny Rogers and Sheena Easton

23.	**How Do You Keep the Music Playing?**	
		James Ingram and Patty Austin
24.	**At Seventeen**	Janis Ian
25.	**Here Come Those Tears Again**	Jackson Browne
26.	**Never Gonna Fall in Love Again**	Eric Carmen
27.	**You Are Everything**	The Stylistics
28.	**The Worst That Could Happen**	The Brooklyn Bridge
29.	**Stranger On the Shore**	Acker Bilk
30.	**Summer, Highland Falls**	Billy Joel
31.	**Time in a Bottle**	Jim Croce
32.	**Fire and Rain**	James Taylor
33.	**Only Wounded**	Peter Allen
34.	**99**	Toto
35.	**In the Air Tonight**	Phil Collins
36.	**Ti Amo**	Laura Branigan
37.	**Fortress Round Your Heart**	Sting
38.	**4th of July, Asbury Park (Sandy)**	Bruce Springsteen
39.	**I'm Not in Love**	10 CC
40.	**You Needed Me**	Anne Murray

Additional runners-up include: Every Country & Western ever written (especially 'She's Acting Single, I'm Drinking Doubles' by Gary Stewart); Bob Seger's 'Hollywood Nights' (Is there anybody who *hasn't* driven along at midnight, depressed over a loved one, listening to this song, debating about driving off the cliff?); Kenny Loggins' 'Heart to Heart' (containing one of the all-time great spurned-love lyrics: 'When you can't give love, you give alibis' . . . also his version of 'You Don't Know Me'); plus any song by Paul Simon (especially 'Trains in the Distance' and 'Sounds of Silence'); Randy Newman (Try listening to 'She's a real emotional girl,' and you'll be convinced life isn't worth living); J. D. Souther; Peter Allen; Don Henley; Steely Dan (avant-garde depression); Michael McDonald (Does anybody have more hurt in his voice? Has anybody been broken up with by more women?); Nat King Cole's 'The Christmas Song' (if they played it on loudspeakers, people would be diving out of sky-scrapers) and finally, Marshall Crenshaw's first album, which is just deliriously heartbreaking – the kind of stuff you hum as you're being indicted for murder.

Of course, once you've moved from depression to anger, an entirely different group of songs comes into play. And although space doesn't permit us to list the entire 'Revenge 100' here, the lyrics of the current no. 1 tune, Martin Briley's 'The Salt in My Tears' are worth mentioning: 'No I won't cry for the wasted years . . .' 'Cause you ain't worth the salt in my tears.'

The End: Starting Over

Going Out in the Material World

'The logic of the human heart is absurd.'
– Julie de Lespinasse, in a letter
dated August 27, 1774.

It was another glorious Saturday evening in London: The streets were awash with taxis; there were a hundred glittering celebrations in progress; a thousand black-tie affairs and countless intimate, romantic dinner parties about to begin.

Not having been invited to any of them, I found myself going down to the local cash card machine shortly after midnight to make a withdrawal for the next week.

'It may not be the most scintillating way to spend a Saturday night,' I told myself, turning the corner, 'but at least it gets you out of the house, which hoovering doesn't.'

As I stood in line behind two sniffling young men who were obtaining funds to purchase a certain Colombian agricultural product, I saw her enter. She was tall and lanky, with a fair face and the kind of sunny blue eyes that appeared as if they'd never looked at anyone with less than kindness. She was wearing worn blue jeans and dirty white running shoes and had a heavy fur coat pulled up tight around her neck. I watched as she moved past a promotional display of free toasters, electric irons, and weekends in Paris that had a sign overhead proclaiming 'The World Is Your Oyster.' She stood in line next to me.

I waited a moment, then turned to her.

'Hello,' I said quietly. 'Come here often.'

'No,' she said, casting her eyes to the floor shyly. 'It's my first time. What about you?'

'I guess I'm a regular,' I told her. 'I live in the area. I'm practically on a first-name basis with the machines.'

I looked in her eyes for a glimmer of hope, but she glanced away, towards the window.

'I'm supposed to meet a friend here,' she said, and began to finger her plastic cash card nervously.

'Me too,' I lied. I wanted to reassure her that I wasn't some kind of urban axe-murderer who preys on innocent women at banking machines on Saturday nights. I also didn't want her to think I was the kind of bloke who went to banking machines on Saturday nights simply because it was better than hoovering.

As she stood there, looking at everything in the room except me, I felt my heart begin to sink as low as the balance in my current account. I decided to plunge on.

'Generally, I hate coming to places like this,' I told her. 'I mean, they're so cold and impersonal. You get the feeling that nobody's interested in getting to know the real you. You're just another name and number.'

She glanced at me out of the corner of an eye. A co-conspiratorial grin began to form in the small of her mouth.

'I know what you mean,' she said. 'No matter what they say, people come here for only one thing. It's so callous. In and out. Almost like . . . like a cash transaction.'

Now it was my turn to glance from the corner of an eye.

'Exactly,' I began to say, but before I could finish I was drowned out by the wail of an approaching police siren. At the machine, the two sniffling young men froze in a cold panic, waited for the warble to pass, and then continued to extract ten pound notes from the wall.

I motioned to her card. 'So what's your secret code?'

She looked to see if the young entrepreneurs were almost finished with their business. At the rate they were going, we stood a good chance of still being there Monday morning at 9:30 when the bank opened.

'Daisy,' she said, turning back to face me. 'For Daisy Buchanan.' She looked at the machine a second time, where the two men were discussing the merits of getting a receipt for tax purposes. 'What's yours?'

For a moment I said nothing. Some coincidences are so good they leave you Dead On Arrival.

'Jay,' I said, and watched as a look of skepticism rolled over her face like thunderclouds moving in on the city in a fast-frame film. I looked at her helplessly. 'It's after my grandfather,' I explained, and waited half a second before I added, 'He was a stock swindler.'

Even standing under the cold fluorescent lighting in January at midnight, her smile was as wide and bright as midday in July.

'So listen,' I teased, 'as long as we're both standing here, can I get you anything from the machine?'

'No thanks,' she said, the laughter lines still dancing on either side of her mouth. 'I'm fine.'

Their high finance concluded, the two commodities brokers ambled towards the door, a blur of dark coats and black beards.

'It's your turn,' she said, adding, 'That is, if there's anything left.'

'Ladies first,' I insisted.

As she stood there with her back towards me, punching away at the machine, working out her debits and balances, working out the business of her life, I began to think about my own transactions.

I thought about all the advice I'd read or received, all the rules and fair warnings. I thought about the way someone yelled at the waiter on a first date, a woman who said 'I love you, I need you, and I want to see you, but have dates every night this week,' and I heard the counterfeit ring of the words 'He's only a friend.'

But then I thought about London in the snow. The first blush of dawn over Regent's Park. Green carrier bags from Harrods. I thought about the black satin lapel of a dinner jacket; pink orchids on a dressing table, the smell of perfume in darkness, and a pair of white tennis socks with fuzzy little balls at the ankles lying at the bottom of a brass bed.

'If you meet the right person,' a friend said, 'the kindred soul with the soft eyes, the knowing glance, and the sigh of compatibility' – I'm pretty sure those were his exact words – 'she can be divorced six times, have a yapping poodle, and summon the waiter with a hand grenade, and none of it matters.'

Two hundred years after Julie de Lespinasse wrote 'The logic of the human heart is absurd,' the patient's condition remains unchanged.

There is always hope, I thought.

There is love at first sight.

There must be somebody out there for everybody.

Why else would God have created those green carrier bags from Harrod's in the first place?

'I'm finished,' she said, walking away from the machine. 'It was nice to meet you.'

I touched her sleeve. 'Look,' I said, 'the truth is that I lied. It's twelve-thirty on a Saturday night, and I'm not going to meet anybody.' I stammered for air. The seconds seemed to pass as if I was waiting for a cheque to clear. 'Would you like to go for a drink?'

She dug her hands into her pockets and scuffed a worn training shoe along the floor.

'I'm sorry,' she said, tilting her head at the angle someone uses when they're about to break up with you, 'but I really am supposed to meet somebody.'

Somewhere in the far, far distance, I could have sworn I heard a cheque of mine bouncing.

Then she looked at her watch.

'But if he hasn't shown up by now, he probably isn't going to.'

'Do you want to have some coffee?'

'Sure,' she said. It was midday in July again. 'Why not?'

Finished with my business at the machine, the two of us walked to the door.

'The world is your oyster,' she sighed, reading the sign above the electric toasters.

'No,' I corrected her. 'The world is actually a giant meeting place.'

Outside, a flotilla of sleepy-eyed taxis cruised silently up Piccadilly. The night was fresh; the buildings sparkled; the streetlamps bathed us in hazy pools of orange light.

'Take my arm,' I whispered in the soft fur of her collar. 'And for a moment – just a moment – let's pretend we're in love.'

'Hey, I've got a question.'

'What's that?'

'How can you be so damn hopeful about this stuff? I know for a fact you haven't had a decent relationship in years. How do you know what a good one is anymore?'

'It's easy. The heart may be dead, but the mind remembers.'

Fontana Paperbacks
Non-fiction

Fontana is a leading paperback publisher of non-fiction.
Below are some recent titles.

- ☐ All in a Day's Work *Danny Danziger* £3.50
- ☐ Policeman's Gazette *Harry Cole* £2.95
- ☐ The Caring Trap *Jenny Pulling* £2.95
- ☐ I Fly Out with Bright Feathers *Allegra Taylor* £3.95
- ☐ Managing Change and Making it Stick *Roger Plant* £3.50
- ☐ Staying Vegetarian *Lynne Alexander* £3.95
- ☐ The Aforesaid Child *Clare Sullivan* £2.95
- ☐ A Grain of Truth *Jack Webster* £2.95
- ☐ John Timpson's Early Morning Book
    John Timpson £3.95
- ☐ Negotiate to Close *Gary Karrass* £3.95
- ☐ Re-making Love *Barbara Ehrereich* £3.95
- ☐ Steve McQueen *Penina Spiegel* £3.95
- ☐ A Vet for All Seasons *Hugh Lasgarn* £2.95
- ☐ Holding the Reins *Juliet Solomon* £3.95
- ☐ Another Voice *Auberon Waugh* £3.95
- ☐ Beyond Fear *Dorothy Rowe* £4.95
- ☐ A Dictionary of Twentieth Century Quotations
    Nigel Rees £4.95
- ☐ Another Bloody Tour *Frances Edmonds* £2.50
- ☐ The Book of Literary Firsts *Nicholas Parsons* £3.95

You can buy Fontana paperbacks at your local bookshop or newsagent.
Or you can order them from Fontana Paperbacks, Cash Sales
Department, Box 29, Douglas, Isle of Man. Please send a cheque, postal
or money order (not currency) worth the purchase price plus 22p per book
for postage (maximum postage required is £3).

NAME (Block letters) _____

ADDRESS _____

_____

_____